voices reading

Grade 5

Facing Choices

Senior Authors

Catherine Snow, Ph.D.
Robert L. Selman, Ph.D.
Patrick C. Walker, Ph.D.

Consulting Authors

Maria Carlo, Ph.D.
Cynthia Tyson, Ph.D.
Arnetha Ball, Ph.D.

ZB Zaner-Bloser

Senior Authors
Catherine Snow, Ph.D.
Henry Lee Shattuck Professor of Human Development and Education,
Harvard Graduate School of Education

Robert L. Selman, Ph.D.
Roy Edward Larsen Professor of Human Development and Education,
Harvard Graduate School of Education

Patrick C. Walker, Ph.D.
Founder, *Voices Literature and Character Education* and *Voices School Design*

Consulting Authors
Maria Carlo, Ph.D.
ELL Specialist

Cynthia Tyson, Ph.D.
Multicultural Literature, Social Studies, and Urban Education Specialist

Arnetha Ball, Ph.D.
Writing Specialist

Reviewer
Barbara Ann Marinak, Ph.D.
Assistant Professor
Millersville University

Editorial Development and Production
Zaner-Bloser, Inc., in collaboration with Nieman Inc. and Ronan Design

ISBN-13: 978-0-7367-5245-9
ISBN-10: 0-7367-5245-5

Zaner-Bloser, Inc., P.O. Box 16764, Columbus, Ohio 43216-6764
1-800-421-3018, www.zaner-bloser.com

Printed in the United States of America   07 08 09 10 11 13880 5 4 3 2 1

Comprehension Strategy:
Take Perspectives

WEEK **1**

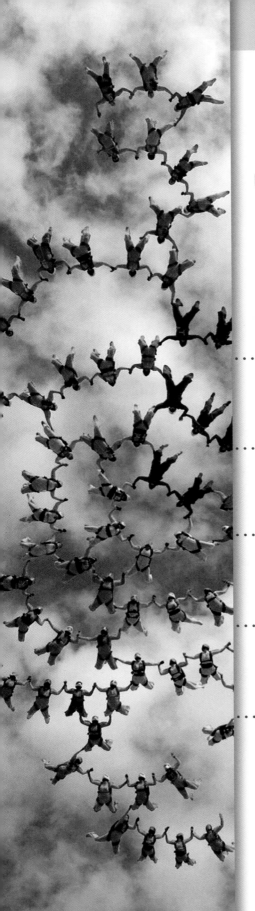

Integrity 114

Courage—and the support of our communities—gives us
strength to take risks.

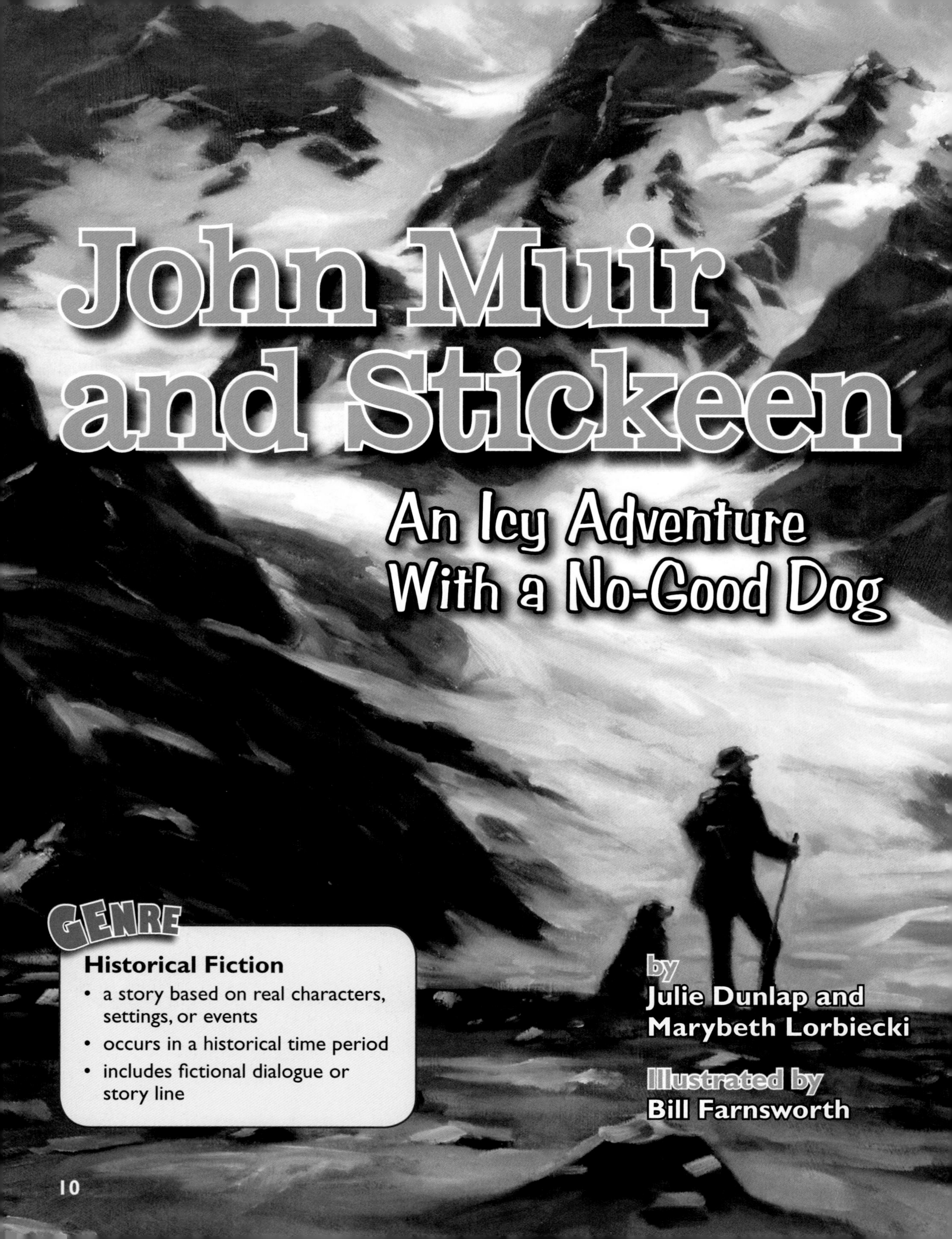

John Muir and Stickeen

An Icy Adventure With a No-Good Dog

by
**Julie Dunlap and
Marybeth Lorbiecki**

Illustrated by
Bill Farnsworth

GENRE

Historical Fiction

- a story based on real characters, settings, or events
- occurs in a historical time period
- includes fictional dialogue or story line

The last morning in Glacier Bay was as wild and dark as an angry grizzly. Tomorrow, the expedition would have to turn for home. The ice called to Muir, rousing him from a deep sleep. He slipped from the tent, careful not to wake the others or Stickeen.

Not far from camp, John spotted a shadow slipping behind him through the trees.

"Go back to camp and have yer breakfast!" John yelled. "This storm will kill ye!"

But Muir should have known. Stickeen was more stubborn than he. Beaten, John offered the drenched dog a bit of his biscuit.

John hiked up rocky slopes, leaving the dog to do as he wished. A shaft of sun split the storm. Ahead stood the king of glaciers!

Hacking ice-steps with his ax, Muir climbed the blue wall. Stickeen scrambled after. On top, an endless sheet of ice stretched before them.

John hiked and sketched for hours, with an eye on the sky. He skipped over small ice cracks and zigzagged around deep crevasses. Stickeen followed.

The clouds blackened again. Muir had to hurry back to camp or face a night on the glacier without tent or fire. He ran hard through the swarming snow, the dog close at his heels. Both were hungry, soaked, and aching from cold.

Then John stopped. Stickeen looked up at him. It was as if the dog knew.

Muir was lost.

Backtracking, John used lines in the ice and wind direction to find his way. Stickeen tracked him like a trooper. At one broad gash, Muir peered down, down, down. Only one spot was narrow enough to leap across. And the far side was much lower. If he jumped down, he could never jump back up.

John hurdled across and down, wobbling on the slippery edge. Stickeen landed after Muir, not a hair to spare. But he trotted on, unrattled. Did nothing scare this dog?

Within minutes, the widest crack yet blocked their way. They were marooned on an island of ice.

Kneeling, John saw one slim chance of escape. Far below, a sagging sliver of ice bridged the chasm. Could it hold their weight?

Stickeen nudged his shoulder. "Hush yer fears, wee beastie," John crooned softly.

Chip, chip, chip. He carved one heel hold, then another, down the ice-canyon's wall.

Ever so slowly, Muir lowered his body onto the sagging bridge.

It held.

Stickeen paced the rim. He began to whimper.

Legs dangling, John shaved flat the ice before him. He hitched himself forward, smoothing a path two-paws wide.

Mournful cries called to him from above.

Somehow, John's cold-clumsy hands cut a ladder up the other side of the canyon and he hauled himself out of danger. But he didn't rejoice.

He looked back for the dog. Could that pitiful creature, wailing and pacing, be Stickeen? "Come on, come on," Muir pleaded. "Ye can do it, wee boy!"

Then Stickeen lay down. His howls dipped and screeched.

John tried ordering him. "Stop yer nonsense!"

Shaking, Stickeen replied with more miserable wails.

Time was running out. With nightfall, Stickeen would likely fall or freeze to death. Could John return to camp for help and grope his way back in the dark?

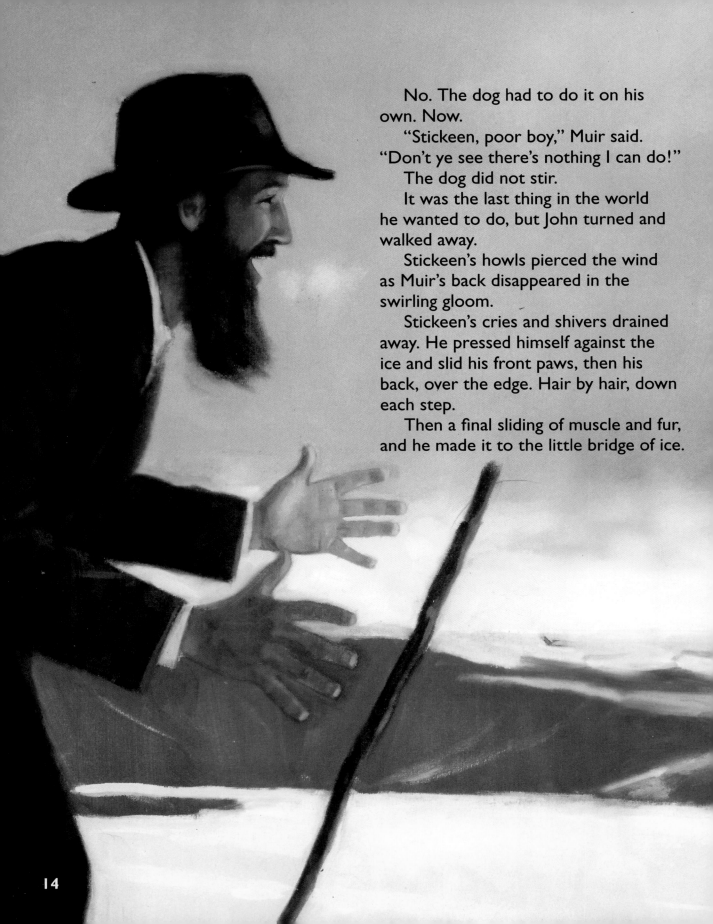

No. The dog had to do it on his own. Now.

"Stickeen, poor boy," Muir said. "Don't ye see there's nothing I can do!"

The dog did not stir.

It was the last thing in the world he wanted to do, but John turned and walked away.

Stickeen's howls pierced the wind as Muir's back disappeared in the swirling gloom.

Stickeen's cries and shivers drained away. He pressed himself against the ice and slid his front paws, then his back, over the edge. Hair by hair, down each step.

Then a final sliding of muscle and fur, and he made it to the little bridge of ice.

But how far he still had to go! His tail fell to half mast. His body began to shake, more fiercely than before. The wind sharpened, nearly pushing Stickeen off the ice bridge.

Then the dog glanced up at the rim.

John was peering down. He had never really left.

The dog's tail flew over his back. Steady as the pelting snow, Stickeen moved over John's bridge-way path.

But at the wall, Stickeen stopped and eyed the towering cliff. Dogs are poor climbers, John knew.

Would Stickeen try?

Stickeen launched skyward, scrabbling up the wall and over the top.

"Well done," John cheered. "Well done, my boy!" He reached out for the dog, but Stickeen whizzed past, whirling, dancing, rolling head over heels. Squealing, the dog spun and charged at John, nearly knocking him down. A gleam in Stickeen's eyes shouted, "Saved! Saved at last!"

Nothing could frighten them now. All the cracks they met seemed puny and easily hopped.

Comprehension Check

Strategy: **Take Perspectives**
How does John's outlook help Stickeen act courageously?

Skill: **Analyze Characters' Conflicts**
Describe how the characters in the story overcome their conflicts.

AMISTAD RISING

A STORY OF FREEDOM

BY VERONICA CHAMBERS
ILLUSTRATED BY PAUL LEE

Cinqué (sĭng′ kā)

During the first two months of his captivity, Cinqué was disturbed to find that he had begun to forget little things about Africa—the smell of freshly harvested rice, the color of the sunsets, the feel of wet grass beneath his running feet. When he closed his eyes, he could see these things only as distant and blurry as a dream. But he could never forget the people he had left behind. His wife. His three children. His mother and father.

Every day Cinqué grew more restless, wondering what the Spaniards intended to do with him and the other Africans. Though they were forbidden to speak, his companions whispered questions: What lay ahead? What would slavery mean? Would they simply be transported from ship to ship indefinitely?

Cinqué had to find out.

Occasionally, a few captives were allowed on deck for some air. Cinqué waited for his turn, and when he was finally ushered above, he attempted to coax some answers from Celestino, the cook. The two men communicated with hand gestures, for neither spoke the other's language.

Cinqué demanded to know what would happen to them.

Celestino smiled devilishly, intent on playing a cruel joke. He pointed to barrels of beef and signaled to Cinqué that the slave traders planned to kill the Africans, cut them up, salt them for preservation, and eat them like cured beef.

Fear and anger filled Cinqué. He would not be eaten by the white men who held him captive. He would not.

He decided to strike that night. With a loose nail he had found earlier in a deck board, he picked the lock on his shackles, freeing himself and then the other prisoners. Once free, they quieted the four children and searched the cargo hold. A box of sugarcane knives was discovered—a boon!

Sneaking up to the deck, they took the crew by surprise. In the fight, Celestino, the captain, and one African were killed. Two of the crew jumped overboard. Three were taken prisoner. Cinqué needed them to navigate the ship back toward Africa, back toward home. When the sun rose again, Cinqué and his companions greeted the day as free people.

But they had claimed victory too soon.

Cinqué ordered the Spaniards to steer the ship toward the rising sun. They obeyed and sailed the ship east toward Africa during the day, but then at night turned the ship around and sailed northwest toward North America. For two months the ship pitched back and forth across the Atlantic Ocean. Nine more Africans died during that time—some from their battle wounds, some from food poisoning, and some from starvation.

Then, on August 27, 1839, the *Amistad* was escorted by an American ship into the harbor of New London, Connecticut. Weary, hungry, and hopelessly lost, Cinqué and the others were forced to come ashore.

An American naval lieutenant saw the possibility for quick profits in the Africans. But this was the North, and a group of whites and free blacks campaigning against the institution of slavery was gaining popularity. They called themselves abolitionists, and they took on Cinqué and the other Africans as their most important case.

The Africans were sent to prison in New Haven, Connecticut, until a decision could be made.

The abolitionists managed to find a translator, and Cinqué told his story in a U.S. court. He was only twenty-five years old, but his experience on the *Amistad* had given him the confidence of a much older man.

The courtroom was crowded, and many were moved by Cinqué's impassioned words.

"I am not here to argue the case against slavery," Cinqué said, "though I will say it is a sin against man and God.

I am here to argue the facts. The indisputable, international law is that the stealing of slaves from Africa is now illegal."

"The men who kidnapped us, who beat and tortured us, were— and are—guilty of this crime," Cinqué continued.

"We are a peaceful people. We regret the loss of life caused by our mutiny. But we are not savages. We took over the ship to save our lives. We have done no wrong. Allow us to go home."

The weekend before the judge made his decision, Cinqué and his companions waited in the New Haven jail, their hearts filled with fear and hope. The judge held the power to make the Africans slaves or to set them free. On Monday morning, January 13, 1840, they worried no longer. He had decided they should be returned home.

They were free.

Strategy: Take Perspectives
How does Cinqué's memory of Africa inspire him to fight the slave traders?

Skill: Recognize Traits of a Character
What traits does Cinqué have that help him achieve freedom?

IT TOOK COURAGE

by Guadalupe V. Lopez

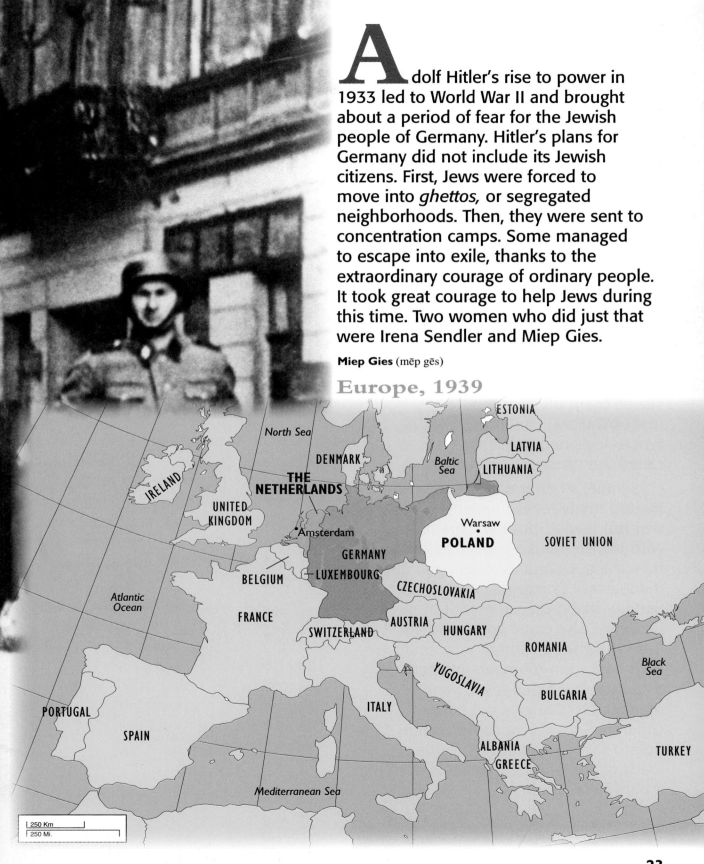

A

dolf Hitler's rise to power in 1933 led to World War II and brought about a period of fear for the Jewish people of Germany. Hitler's plans for Germany did not include its Jewish citizens. First, Jews were forced to move into *ghettos,* or segregated neighborhoods. Then, they were sent to concentration camps. Some managed to escape into exile, thanks to the extraordinary courage of ordinary people. It took great courage to help Jews during this time. Two women who did just that were Irena Sendler and Miep Gies.

Miep Gies (mēp gēs)

Europe, 1939

North Sea

ESTONIA

LATVIA

DENMARK

Baltic Sea

LITHUANIA

IRELAND

THE NETHERLANDS

UNITED KINGDOM

·Amsterdam

Warsaw
·
POLAND

SOVIET UNION

GERMANY

BELGIUM — LUXEMBOURG

CZECHOSLOVAKIA

Atlantic Ocean

FRANCE

SWITZERLAND

AUSTRIA

HUNGARY

ROMANIA

Black Sea

YUGOSLAVIA

BULGARIA

PORTUGAL

ITALY

SPAIN

ALBANIA

GREECE

TURKEY

Mediterranean Sea

250 Km
250 Mi.

Irena Sendler

Irena Sendler was a Polish woman who worked in the Warsaw Social Welfare Department. Warsaw, the capital of Poland, was a bustling center of Jewish activity. This made it a prime target for the Nazis, Hitler's followers. When the Nazis occupied Warsaw in 1939, they ordered that all Jews be taken to one area in Warsaw. Here, the Nazis held Jews captive and sealed them off from the rest of Warsaw. The place where Jews had to live was called the Warsaw Ghetto.

Irena Sendler after the performance of *Life in a Jar*, the play inspired by her story

Sendler's father was a doctor who treated many Jewish patients. Sendler was not Jewish, but her experiences with Jewish people convinced her to help them. German soldiers guarded the Warsaw Ghetto day and night, but Sendler had a special permit through her work. She could come and go from the ghetto without a problem. With help from members of Zegota, a council that aided Jews, Sendler managed to smuggle out some children. Some were carried out in potato sacks. Others were hidden in loads of goods. One mechanic even hid a baby in his toolbox.

Zegota (zĕ′ gə tä)

Sendler, a young mother herself, knew how heartbreaking it was for the Jewish mothers to give up their children. She tried to comfort the mothers. Then she took the children to non-Jewish families for their own protection. Sendler gave the children false names and family histories, which the older children had to memorize.

Sendler did not want the children to forget who they were, so she noted their birth names with their new identities. She stashed these valuable facts inside glass jars, which she buried in a neighbor's garden. Eventually, Sendler's jars contained the names of about 2,500 children who had been saved. After the war, she retrieved the jars and reunited as many families as she could.

In 2001, when Sendler was 91 years old, a group of high school drama students and their teacher visited her. They had developed a presentation inspired by her noble deeds. This prize-winning presentation was entitled *Life in a Jar*, and it told Irena Sendler's story to the world.

Miep Gies

In Amsterdam, the Netherlands, a young Jewish girl named Anne Frank kept a diary in which she described how her family was taken from their home and smuggled into hiding from the Nazis. Miep Gies, an employee and friend of Anne's father, helped hide the Frank family.

Miep Gies, 1935

Gies brought the family food, water, and, most important, friendship. Over time, Gies became particularly close to Anne. Gies supplied Anne with blank accounting books and encouraged her to keep writing. She also bought Anne her first pair of high-heeled shoes.

For two years, Miep Gies helped keep the Frank family hidden. Unfortunately, the Nazis eventually discovered the hiding place and arrested everyone.

Anne Frank writes at her desk in 1941.

All those in hiding were sent to concentration camps. Gies, who was not there the day the Nazis raided the hiding place, went back to the little room and discovered Anne's precious diary amid the debris. She hid it in a locked drawer for a year.

When Gies received the terrible news that Anne had died, she gave the diary to Anne's father, Otto. Otto was the only member of the Frank family to survive the war. In 1947, he published Anne's diary. Those who read it were touched by Anne's story. Gies became a celebrity in the Netherlands and received many awards. She was knighted by Queen Beatrix of the Netherlands in 1997 for her courage and integrity.

Both Irena Sendler and Miep Gies insisted that they were only ordinary women, and both wished they could have done more.

Comprehension Check

Strategy: **Take Perspectives**
Why did Irena Sendler and Miep Gies choose to help Jewish people during World War II?

Skill: **Sequence/Chronological Order**
What events forced Jews in Europe to go into hiding during World War II?

GENRE

Poetry

- a form of writing often broken into verses, lines, and stanzas
- uses imaginative language and sensory details
- may include rhyme, rhythm, alliteration, or shape

LIFE DOESN'T FRIGHTEN ME

Poem by Maya Angelou

Shadows on the wall
Noises down the hall
Life doesn't frighten me at all
Bad dogs barking loud
Big ghosts in a cloud
Life doesn't frighten me at all.

Mean old Mother Goose
Lions on the loose
They don't frighten me at all
Dragons breathing flame
On my counterpane
That doesn't frighten me at all,

I go boo
Make them shoo
I make fun
Way they run
I won't cry
So they fly
I just smile
They go wild
Life doesn't frighten me at all.

Tough guys in a fight
All alone at night
Life doesn't frighten me at all.
Panthers in the park
Strangers in the dark
No, they don't frighten me at all.

That new classroom where
Boys all pull my hair
(Kissy little girls
With their hair in curls)
They don't frighten me at all.

Don't show me frogs and snakes
And listen for my scream,
If I'm afraid at all
It's only in my dreams.

I've got a magic charm
That I keep up my sleeve,
I can walk the ocean floor
And never have to breathe.

Life doesn't frighten me at all
Not at all
Not at all.
Life doesn't frighten me at all.

Comprehension Check

Strategy: **Take Perspectives**
How does the speaker of the poem describe life?

Skill: **Identify Sound Devices: Rhyme, Rhythm**
Describe the rhyming pattern in the poem.

Walking Iron

by Tamim Ansary

They move about on thin rails, high above the city streets, where one careless step could send them falling hundreds of feet to their deaths! These are the Mohawk ironworkers, building a skyscraper—a job they call "walking iron."

GENRE

Informational Article
- a short piece of factual writing that offers explanations about a topic
- provides real-world examples
- often includes maps, charts, and graphs

The Fearless Wonders

Most major cities now have towering buildings known as skyscrapers. These gigantic structures are built around metal frames that look like monkey bars. Who built those incredible forms? Someone had to climb those harrowing frames and weld the rails together with melted iron. Over the years, many of those workers have been Mohawk Native Americans.

The Mohawks live in the northeastern United States. In 1850, the Grand Trunk Railway hired Mohawks for one of its major construction projects: building the Victoria Bridge over the Saint Lawrence River.

As the Mohawk workers confidently walked the frame of the huge iron bridge, one of the work crew bosses noticed something. The Mohawks showed no fear of heights. Any job they could do on the ground, they could do just as well high above ground.

Word spread, and the company decided to teach 12 Mohawk teenagers how to work with iron. These 12, who came to be known as "the fearless wonders" and later as "skywalkers," trained other Mohawks to work with iron.

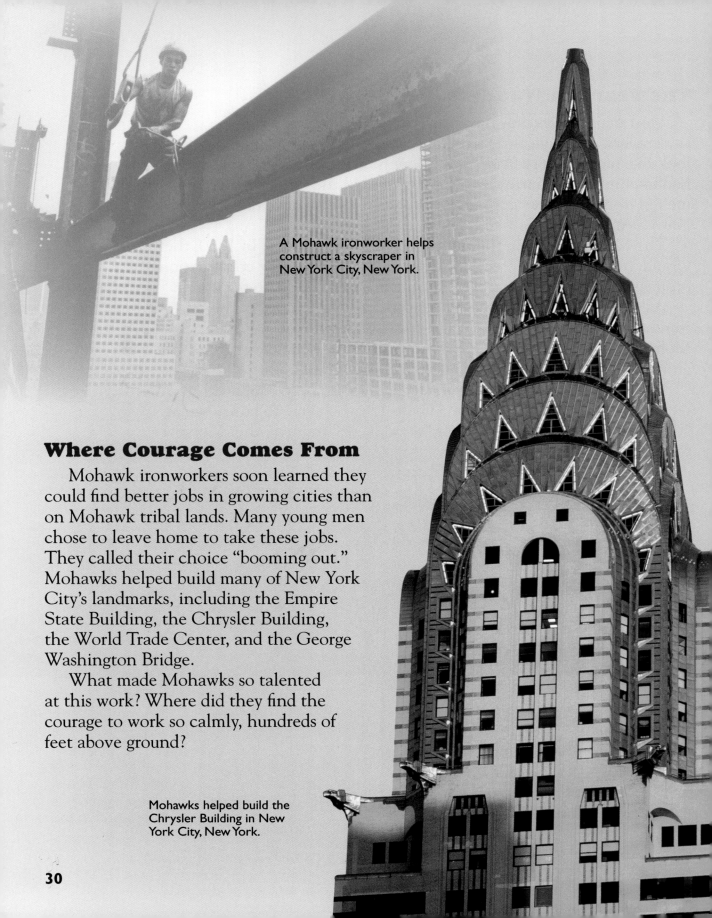

A Mohawk ironworker helps construct a skyscraper in New York City, New York.

Where Courage Comes From

Mohawk ironworkers soon learned they could find better jobs in growing cities than on Mohawk tribal lands. Many young men chose to leave home to take these jobs. They called their choice "booming out." Mohawks helped build many of New York City's landmarks, including the Empire State Building, the Chrysler Building, the World Trade Center, and the George Washington Bridge.

What made Mohawks so talented at this work? Where did they find the courage to work so calmly, hundreds of feet above ground?

Mohawks helped build the Chrysler Building in New York City, New York.

They elicited courage from each other. The Mohawk way of life was very different from urban life. When Mohawks "boomed out," they discovered themselves among strangers, which led the young men to draw closer to one another. After work, they got together to sing their own songs and tell stories about their ancestors.

Confronting Fear

In ancient times, Mohawks had been hunters. They admired courage because they needed that trait to survive. Mohawk boys grew up longing to prove themselves through brave deeds.

At the beginning of the 20th century, in an expanding nation, Mohawks found jobs that required great courage. These young men wanted to earn each other's respect and to make their families and ancestors proud as well. They "walked iron" in spite of the fear they felt.

Kyle Karonhiaktatie Beauvais is a Mohawk ironworker. He says, "A lot of people think Mohawks aren't afraid of heights; that's not true. We have as much fear as the next guy. The difference is we deal with it better. We also have the experience of the old-timers to follow and the responsibility to lead the younger guys. There's pride in walking iron."

The courage of Mohawk ironworkers still shapes New York. Crews continue to build immense skyscrapers, one day at a time, walking the iron. Their contributions are ever-present along New York's skyline.

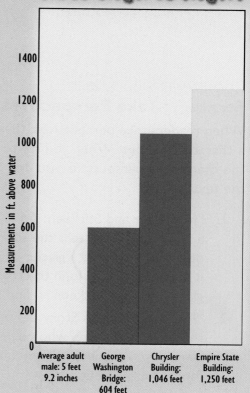

How High Is High?

Measurements in ft. above water

- Average adult male: 5 feet 9.2 inches
- George Washington Bridge: 604 feet
- Chrysler Building: 1,046 feet
- Empire State Building: 1,250 feet

Comprehension Check

Strategy: **Take Perspectives**
Imagine that you are a Mohawk ironworker. List the ways your job is right for you.

Skill: **Author's Viewpoint**
What does the author think about the Mohawk ironworkers?

React and Respond

Comprehension Check
Strategy: Take Perspectives

When readers take perspectives, they put themselves into a character's shoes. When you try to see the world from the character's perspective, you find deeper meaning in the text.

1. "John Muir and Stickeen: An Icy Adventure With a No-Good Dog" tells the story of John and his dog, who explored a glacier together. Why was it so important to John to cross the crack in the glacier, leaving Stickeen to find his own way?

2. "Amistad Rising: A Story of Freedom" recounts the story of Cinqué, who helped overtake a slave ship. Why was it important that Cinqué fought for his freedom?

3. "It Took Courage" introduces two women, Irena Sendler and Miep Gies, who took risks to help Jewish families during World War II. How did having her own family influence Sendler to help Jewish families?

4. "Life Doesn't Frighten Me" lists many things that could scare a person. Why do you think life doesn't frighten the speaker at all?

5. "Walking Iron" describes Mohawk ironworkers and their ability to build tall bridges and skyscrapers. What do the Mohawk ironworkers think about being hired for such dangerous jobs?

Compare Texts
Make a Venn Diagram

Use a Venn Diagram to compare and contrast how the characters in a selection show courage. Consider how Miep Gies and Irena Sendler showed courage in different ways. For example, Irena Sendler's work enabled her to help several children, whereas Miep Gies focused on helping the Franks, a particular family she had befriended.

Now, make your own Venn Diagram on a separate sheet of paper. Compare the ways Cinqué from "Amistad Rising" and John Muir from "John Muir and Stickeen" show courage.

Courageous Characters

Irena Sendler
- used her work permit to secretly help Jews
- took Jewish children to live with non-Jewish families for protection
- reunited families after the war

Both
- risked their lives to help Jews during World War II

Miep Gies
- helped hide the Frank family
- rescued Anne Frank's diary, which would later be published

Character Development
Courage

Courage—and the support of our communities—gives us strength to take risks.

Think about a time when you took a risk. Put your thoughts in a 5 W's Chart. Copy the chart below.

Taking Risks	
What happened?	
Who was there?	
Why did it happen?	
When did it happen?	
Where did it happen?	

Technology
Courageous Jobs

There are many dangerous jobs in our society. For example, the job of a firefighter requires a lot of courage. Check out PBS at **www.pbs.org/ testofcourage/** to find out more.

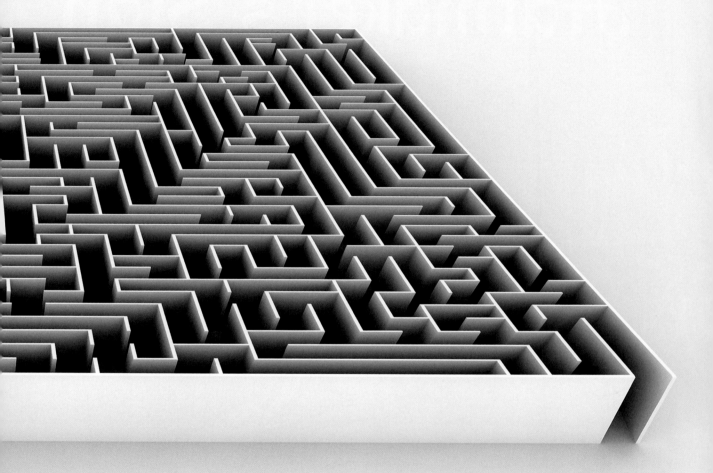

The Hatmaker's Sign

A Story by Benjamin Franklin

Retold by Candace Fleming   *Illustrated by Robert Andrew Parker*

GENRE

Historical Fiction
- a story based on real characters, settings, or events
- occurs in a historical time period
- includes fictional dialogue or story line

Knee-deep in used parchment and broken quill pens, John struggled to create a sign for his shop. And at long last, he wrote one. It read:

John Thompson, Hatmaker
Fashionable Hats Sold Inside For Ready Money

Beneath the words, John drew a picture of a hat.

"It is exactly right," John exclaimed. "Customers will surely love it."

But before hurrying to the sign maker's shop, where his words and picture would be painted onto board, John showed his parchment to his wife, Hannah.

"Oh John," Hannah giggled after reading what John had written. "Why bother with the words 'for ready money'? You're not going to sell hats for anything else, are you? Remove those words and your sign will be perfect."

"You're probably right," sighed John.

So John rewrote his sign. Now it read:

John Thompson, Hatmaker
Fashionable Hats Sold Inside

Beneath the words he drew a picture of a hat.

Parchment in hand, John headed for the sign maker's shop.

He had gone as far as the Old North Church when he met Reverend Brimstone.

"Where are you strolling on such a fine morning?" asked the reverend.

"To the sign maker's shop," replied John. He held out his parchment.

Reverend Brimstone read it.

"May I make a suggestion?" he asked. "Why don't you take out the words 'John Thompson, Hatmaker'? After all, customers won't care who made the hats as long as they are good ones."

"You're probably right," sighed John.

And after tipping his tricorn to the reverend, John hurried back to his hat shop and rewrote his sign. Now it read:

Fashionable Hats Sold Inside

Beneath the words he drew a picture of a hat.

Parchment in hand, John headed for the sign maker's shop.

He had gone as far as Beacon Hill when Lady Manderly stepped from her carriage and into his path.

"What have you there?" asked the haughty lady. She plucked the parchment from John's hand and read it.

"Absurd!" she snorted. "Why bother with the word 'fashionable'? Do you intend to sell unfashionable hats?"

"Absolutely not!" cried John.

"Then strike that word out," replied Lady Manderly. "Without it, your sign will be perfect."

"You are probably right," sighed John.

And after kissing the lady's elegantly gloved hand, John hurried back to his shop and rewrote his sign. Now it read:

Hats Sold Inside

Beneath the words he drew a picture of a hat.

Parchment in hand, John headed for the sign maker's shop.

He had gone as far as Boston Common when he met a British magistrate.

The magistrate, always on the lookout for unlawful behavior, eyed John's parchment.

"Hand it over or face the stockades!" demanded the magistrate.

John did. He gulped nervously as the magistrate read it.

"Tell me hatter," bullied the magistrate. "Why do you write 'sold inside'? Are you planning on selling your hats from the street? That is against the law, you know. I say delete those words if you want to stay out of jail. And if you want your sign to be perfect."

"Yes, sir. No, sir. I mean I will, sir," stammered John.

And after hastily bowing to the magistrate, John hurried back to his hat shop and rewrote his sign. Now it read:

Hats

Beneath the word he drew a picture of a hat.

Parchment in hand, John headed for the sign maker's shop.

He had gone as far as the Charles River when a brisk breeze snatched the parchment from his hand and dropped it at the feet of two young apprentices sitting on a crate of tea.

The first apprentice picked up the parchment and read it.

"Hey, mister," he said. "Why do you write 'hats' when you already have a picture of one?"

"Yes, why?" asked the second apprentice.

"It would be a much better sign without that word," suggested the first apprentice.

"It would be perfect," added the second apprentice.

"You are probably right," sighed John.

And after tossing each boy a halfpenny, John hurried back to his hat shop and rewrote his sign. Now it read:

Nothing.

He drew a picture of a hat.

Parchment in hand, John headed for the sign maker's shop.

He had gone as far as Harvard College when he met Professor Wordsworth.

John shoved his parchment under the professor's nose. "Please, sir," he said. "Would you tell me what you think of my sign?"

The surprised professor straightened his spectacles and peered at the picture.

"Since you ask my opinion, I shall give it," said Professor Wordsworth. "However, I must ask you a question first. Are you displaying your hats in your shop's front window?"

John nodded.

"Then this picture is useless," declared the professor. "Everyone will know you sell hats simply by looking in your window. Eliminate the picture and your sign will be perfect."

"You are probably right," sighed John.

And after pumping the professor's hand in thanks, John hurried back to his hat shop and rewrote his sign.

Now it read nothing.

It showed nothing.

It was wordless and pictureless and entirely blank.

Parchment in hand, John headed to the sign maker's shop.

Past the Old North Church and Beacon Hill. Past Boston Common and the wharf and Harvard College.

At long last, John arrived at the sign maker's shop. Exhausted, he handed over his parchment.

"I do not understand," said the puzzled sign maker as he stared at the empty parchment. "What does this mean? What are you trying to say?"

John shrugged. "I do not know anymore," he admitted. And he told the sign maker about his new hat shop, and his sign, and how no one had thought it was perfect enough.

When he had finished, the sign maker said, "May I make a suggestion? How about:

*John Thompson, Hatmaker
Fashionable Hats Sold Inside For Ready Money.'*

"Beneath the words I will draw a picture of a hat."

"Yes!" exclaimed John. "How clever of you to think of it. That is exactly right! Indeed, it's perfect!"

Comprehension Check

Strategy: **Text-to-Text Connections**
How are John's conflicts in this story similar to the characters' conflicts in other stories you have read?

Skill: **Cause and Effect**
What happens to John's sign when he takes everyone's advice?

The Rich Man
and the Shoemaker

Fable by La Fontaine   *Retold and Illustrated by Bernadette Watts*

GENRE

Fable

- a short tale that can be prose or poetry
- includes speaking animals or objects as characters
- teaches a lesson

There once lived, in a very fine city, a shoemaker who sang happily at his work from dawn till dusk.

Across the street from the shoemaker lived a merchant, so rich he rolled in gold. The merchant never sang and slept little, spending every waking hour counting his riches. He was woken up very early by the shoemaker's happy songs, and during the day he would lose count of his calculations, distracted by the singing.

At last he asked the shoemaker to call at his house. "How much do you earn?" he asked the shoemaker.

The shoemaker laughed and shrugged his shoulders. "I struggle each day to earn enough to put food on the table, and little else," he replied.

"I will give you enough gold to put a feast on your table and more for your wife to store. But you must stop singing!" said the merchant.

The shoemaker was shocked and would not agree to such an arrangement. "We can manage very well without your gold, thank you," he said and went home.

The shoemaker went on singing while he worked, and the merchant became more and more irritated.

One day the merchant called at the shoemaker's shop. The shoemaker was delighted, thinking the rich man had come to order a pair of winter boots, and he sprang up to welcome him.

"You must stop singing, so I can count my gold and get some sleep!" said the merchant. "In return here is a purse full of gold pieces for you. You can take a break from your work. Have some easy days."

"But what would I do without my work?" asked the shoemaker in great surprise. "And as for singing . . . why, if I did not sing, I could not work."

So the merchant left and went back to his own cold and lonely home.

Some time later the merchant called on the shoemaker again. The snow lay thick on the street and across the rooftops. The merchant wrapped himself in a rich cloak and hurried across the street.

"Come in!" called the shoemaker. "Don't stand out there in the bitter cold!"

So the merchant stepped into the warm room. "I will give you all the gold you can ever spend and precious stones, too, if only you will stop singing!" And so saying, the merchant took out a chest inlaid with jewels.

The shoemaker was amazed—he had never seen such riches. It is cold, so cold, he thought to himself. With this gold I could buy my wife and children warm coats, scarves, too. And surely there is enough to buy a roast turkey to put on the table, and more coal to put on the fire.

So he agreed with the merchant to take the gold and stop singing.

The merchant, happy for once, hurried home.

Until I have time to go shopping I must hide these riches, thought the shoemaker. He went out into their little garden and dug a hole, which was difficult as the ground was frozen. There he buried the chest.

The disturbed place in the garden was very easily seen. All night the shoemaker could not sleep, but kept looking out the window. The next day he was too anxious to do any work. Night after night he kept watch on the garden, and day after day he was quiet and worried and unable to work.

If the cat by the fire stretched, the shoemaker thought he heard robbers. He thought that the ticking of the clock was someone sneaking around the house. And when his wife drew water, he believed he heard robbers dragging the chest from the ground. Even his children had to tiptoe about and whisper, so they didn't alarm their poor father.

Then one morning the shoemaker's wife said, "Give back the gold. What has it brought except unhappiness?"

So the shoemaker dug up the chest. He carried it across the street and knocked loudly at the rich man's door.

"Give me back my songs and peaceful sleep!" he said. "Here, take your gold and precious gems."

And the shoemaker returned home to his family, a happy man again.

Comprehension Check

Strategy: **Text-to-Text Connections**
How is this story like another fable you have read?

Skill: **Understand and State the Theme**
What does the shoemaker learn in this story?

THE SINGING HAT

by Tohby Riddle

One fine spring day, Colin Jenkins took the time to sit under a tree. He had not rested for a long while, and sleep soon overcame him.

Colin Jenkins slept deeply and longer than his lunch hour. In fact, when he awoke it was dark, so he made his way home.

All the while, he could not help but notice that people looked at him in ways that he had never been looked at before.

What Colin Jenkins did not know was that while he slept under the tree in the park, so deeply and so still, a bird had built a nest on his head. And there it sat like a rare and peculiar crown.

It was not until Colin Jenkins reached home that he became aware of this new development.

Colin Jenkins was now faced with quite a conundrum. He could not easily dislodge the perfectly fitted nest from his head, nor did he want to interrupt the bird at such a fragile and important time of life.

Furthermore, his young daughter urged him to leave the poor bird and its egg alone and added that if he sat still long enough she would help feed it.

Colin Jenkins decided—right there and then—that it was not wise to interfere with nature. Having a bird's nest on his head might cause a problem or two, he thought, but he would bear it, so to speak.

From that day on, Colin Jenkins noticed a new world around him. People divided into two groups: those who didn't seem to mind what he had on his head, and those who did.

Colin Jenkins made some new friends . . . and lost some old ones.

He wasn't welcome where once he was . . . meetings at work took on a different character . . . ordinary occasions did not always remain ordinary.

The bird even made noises as if it were talking.

Life was definitely becoming less usual, Colin Jenkins thought to himself at the end of each day.

One day, Colin Jenkins turned up at work to find he no longer had a job. His boss's reasons for letting him go were not very clear.

Colin Jenkins didn't hear much of it anyway, because an egg was hatching on his head.

"Life goes on," he thought.

As he left the office building for the last time, something from a passing bird spattered on his shoulder.

"I don't suppose I should take this personally," reflected Colin Jenkins, but deep down he knew he'd had better days than this.

The arrival of the baby bird had quite an impact on Colin Jenkins's life.

Feeding times in particular were difficult to ignore.

The young bird's first attempts to fly were also difficult to ignore. Nor did they assist Colin Jenkins when trying to get another job.

CLUNK!

They didn't seem to assist him in any way at all. Without work, Colin Jenkins could no longer afford to keep his home. His landlord, who he'd hoped might be more understanding of people with birds' nests on their heads, wasn't.

Of course, it wasn't just landlords who didn't take kindly to people with birds' nests on their heads. Sometimes Colin Jenkins felt alone. And at these times, not even his daughter seemed able to cheer him.

He decided to take action and return to where this chapter of his life had begun—to the tree under which he'd slept so deeply.

"Maybe I can put this nest in that tree," he hoped. But when he found the tree he noticed that there was already a nest in it. He looked at other trees in the small park . . . It was as if there was no other home for this nest but the top of his head.

"I suppose it has fallen on me to care for this nest," he realized, turning homeward.

"Good heavens, no! It can't be!" exclaimed a man on Colin Jenkins's train. "That bird on your head . . . why, it's possibly the rarest in the world! I thought it had even become extinct!"

The man, who might have been an ornithologist, followed Colin Jenkins out of the train station. "I can't tell you how fortunate it is that these birds are still with us! Not a lot is known about them because sightings are so few. But what we do know . . ."

At that moment the bird took off. The younger bird followed. It seemed to have finally mastered flight, and together the birds soared ever higher into the evening sky.

It looked as if they were gone for good. Colin Jenkins felt a near avalanche of relief. He raised the nest from his head and went to dispose of it.

"Keep the nest," said the man. "The birds have gone, but they may return. That is, if I know my facts about these birds."

Colin Jenkins realized that he was right outside his home. He turned to say farewell to the man who might have been an ornithologist, but he was nowhere to be seen, swallowed up by the rush-hour crowd.

Comprehension Check

Strategy: **Text-to-Text Connections**
How are Colin Jenkins's reactions to others' opinions different from John Thompson's reactions in "The Hatmaker's Sign"?

Skill: **Recognize and Respond to Humor**
What makes this story funny?

Four Who Dared

by Erin Bad Hand

GENRE

Informational Article

- a short piece of factual writing that offers explanations about a topic
- provides real-world examples
- often includes maps, charts, and graphs

Sometimes we encounter opportunities to try something new and possibly scary. When we face these situations, it helps to know how others have faced similar times with courage.

Swimming From Alcatraz

Johnny Wilson of Hillsborough, California, and Braxton Bilbrey of Glendale, Arizona, are average boys. They make choices every day, such as what to eat for breakfast and what to wear. These two boys also have something unusual in common. Both swam from Alcatraz to the San Francisco Aquatic Park, a distance of approximately 1.4 miles. Alcatraz is an island in the San Francisco Bay and a former prison. The boys not only swam the distance, but they did so in the chilly 53°F water with the high waves pushing hard against them.

Many adults swim in this event every year, but Johnny was nine years old when he swam to benefit victims of Hurricane Katrina. Braxton was seven years old when he heard about Johnny's swim and was inspired to try it. Braxton's mother wasn't keen on his swimming such a distance at first. However, Braxton was determined, training for two hours a day, four times a week. His mother finally agreed, and Braxton swam the course with three adults looking out for him. Both of these boys set out to accomplish a goal that most adults would not even attempt. With determination, they succeeded!

Why Alcatraz Island?

Why is swimming from Alcatraz Island to the shore such an achievement? From 1861 to 1963, Alcatraz was a prison, located on an island more than a mile offshore in the San Francisco Bay, in shark-infested waters. Officials claimed no one could escape from it. Prisoners tried to swim away and escape over the years. There are no confirmed survivors, although some believe that a 1962 attempt succeeded. Life vests drifted to shore, but the three men who left Alcatraz on the raft were never found.

Wilson swims across the San Francisco Bay.

Derby Dreams

Kristin Mulhall treats her animals like family members. As a child, she competed in equestrian jumping competitions. At age 19, a serious infection in her arm ended her pursuit of a spot on the Olympic equestrian team. Kristin needed a fresh challenge. She decided to train thoroughbred racehorses. Her ultimate goal was to become one of the youngest female trainers ever to compete in the Kentucky Derby.

Kristin's family did not support her decision at first. They thought it might be too difficult. Kristin continued training her horses, pushing herself to improve. Eventually, she proved to her family and to others that she could hold her own in the tough competition of horseracing. Her dedication to her animals and her tremendous patience impressed competitors. In 2004, Kristin achieved her goal, bringing her horse, Imperialism, to the Kentucky Derby. Despite being partially blind, Imperialism finished third.

Kristin Mulhall trains her horse, Imperialism, in 2004.

Write-In Candidate

Michael Sessions wanted to contribute to his community so much that he decided to run for mayor of his town, Hillsdale, Michigan. This might not be unusual, but Michael was a senior in high school! One week after his 18th birthday, Michael declared himself a write-in candidate for mayor. His father and many other town residents were unemployed, and Michael wanted to help. He devoted himself to his campaign, using money from a summer job to make ads and signs. Michael discovered that it was hard work trying to reach all 9,000 residents of Hillsdale. With help from the local fire department, he set out on his campaign by going door to door.

Finally, Election Day 2005 arrived. When the votes were counted, Michael had won! He defeated the current mayor by two votes, becoming the youngest mayor that Hillsdale, Michigan, had ever elected. He set to work immediately, casting one of nine votes on the City Council. He proved that anyone can make a difference if they work hard enough.

As these stories prove, age is no barrier to success. Set goals, make a plan, and follow through with it. With self-awareness, you can do anything you set your mind to.

Michael Sessions serving as mayor of Hillsdale, Michigan, in 2005

Comprehension Check

Strategy: **Text-to-Text Connections**
What other selections have you read this year that included amazing young people? What do these people have in common?

Skill: **Compare and Contrast**
How was Michael like other mayoral candidates? How was he different?

The Emperor's New Clothes

Based on a fairy tale by **Hans Christian Andersen**

Retold by **Don Abramson**

Characters

Narrator	Prime	Weaver 1
Emperor	Minister	Weaver 2
	Wardrobe	Child
	Master	

Drama

- a story written in the form of a script
- uses stage directions and dialogue to advance the plot
- is written to be performed

Scene 1

NARRATOR: Many years ago in China lived an emperor who was very vain and very fond of new clothes. He had, they said, a passion for fashion. One day, he was scolding his wardrobe master.

EMPEROR: Wardrobe Master, I can't wear that robe to the royal audience. I wore it two years ago. No, no—I must have something new!

NARRATOR: Then one day, two weavers arrived at the palace.

WEAVER 1: Your excellence, we can weave you a cloth unlike any you've ever seen.

WEAVER 2: It will be so light and so delicate, you'll never know you're wearing it.

WEAVER 1: This cloth has a special power—it is invisible to anyone who is unfit for his position.

EMPEROR (to himself): That sounds useful. I can wear something fabulous and find out which officials are not fit to serve me. Wardrobe Master, show these men to the royal workshop. Prime Minister, see that they're well paid for their efforts.

NARRATOR: So the two weavers began their work in the palace. They worked for days at the looms, but they were only pretending to weave a cloth. In reality, they weren't weaving anything at all!

Scene 2

NARRATOR: After a while, the emperor thought to check the weavers' progress. He sent the prime minister to ask about the progress on his new robe.

WEAVER 2: Prime Minister, we are so glad to see you. Here, let us show you this wondrous cloth we're weaving. Yellow, of course—

WEAVER 1: —because only the emperor is allowed to wear yellow.

PRIME MINISTER *(to himself)*: Goodness, I can't see a thing. Am I unfit to serve the emperor? What can I do? *(To EMPEROR)* Excellence, the cloth is truly miraculous. It's unlike anything I've ever seen.

EMPEROR *(to himself)*: Good! I shall have magnificent clothes, which of course I deserve. Because the prime minister saw the cloth, I know he is worthy of his position.

NARRATOR: A week later, the emperor was eager to wear his fine new clothes. This time, he sent the wardrobe master to check on the weavers' progress.

WEAVER 2: Wardrobe Master, we are so glad to see you. Here, look at this!

WEAVER 1: We've sewn the robe, and now we're doing the embroidery. It's a dragon, of course, the symbol of royalty.

WARDROBE MASTER *(to himself)*: Oh, oh. I can't see a thing. I know I'm fit for my position, but what will I say to the emperor? *(To EMPEROR)* Excellence, it is indeed a work of art. The colors are perfect!

EMPEROR: Good! I will wear it in the royal procession next week. *(To himself)* Truly, I am blessed. Beautiful clothes and competent people!

Scene 3

NARRATOR: The big day came. The weavers presented the invisible robe with much ceremony. They helped the emperor undress and then pretended to dress him in the new robe.

EMPEROR *(shocked and to himself)*: Oh dear, I can't see a thing. No bother. My officials have assured me that this is the finest robe ever. I'm still the best-dressed emperor!

NARRATOR: The procession started. Courtiers led the way, followed by the emperor, marching with pride. The townspeople looked on in amazement. The emperor, they saw, was marching in his underwear! No one dared to mention it. No one dared to laugh, although some people hid smiles behind their fans. Before his mother could stop him, however, a small child blurted out—

CHILD: Look—the emperor is in his underwear!

EMPEROR *(startled)*: Prime Minister, aren't I wearing fine yellow robes?

PRIME MINISTER *(to himself)*: What should I say? I put him in this position so I wouldn't seem unfit to serve him. What have I done? *(He pauses, looks unhappy, and then seems to make up his mind. To* EMPEROR*)* Why, Excellence, I—ah—yes, I'm afraid what the child said is true.

EMPEROR: As my trusted advisor, what would you suggest I do?

PRIME MINISTER: Well, I'd say—hold your head up and keep marching.

NARRATOR: And so the emperor did. When he reached the privacy of his royal rooms, however, he did a lot of thinking. Never again, the courtiers noticed, was the emperor quite so vain.

Comprehension Check

Strategy: **Text-to-Text Connections**
How is the emperor's discovery about his mistake similar to something else you have read?

Skill: **Understand Symbolism**
What does the invisible robe represent?

React and Respond

Comprehension Check
Strategy: Text-to-Text Connections

As you read, the text may remind you of another text you have read. When this happens, you make a text-to-text connection. Think about how the characters, events, settings, or other details compare to other texts you have read.

1. In "The Hatmaker's Sign," John receives various opinions about what should be on his sign. What other characters that you have read about show the determination John shows to get something "just right"?

2. "The Rich Man and the Shoemaker" tells the story of a shoemaker who gives up riches for happiness. Describe another story in which a character gives up money for happiness.

3. Colin Jenkins in "The Singing Hat" decides not to remove the bird's nest on his head because he does not want to disturb nature. How is this story like other stories that discuss nature preservation?

4. "Four Who Dared" describes amazing accomplishments of young people. Why is it important to read about people who did amazing things when they were young?

5. "The Emperor's New Clothes" is the story of a vain leader who marches in nothing but his underwear. What lessons have characters learned in other stories?

Compare Texts
Make a Character Traits Chart

When you compare the characters from the selections you read, you see how they are alike and different. Use a Character Traits Chart like the one below to organize each character's traits. The chart below includes information about John from "The Hatmaker's Sign." Make your own chart and record your observations about the other characters' traits.

Character	Title	What Character Looks Like	How Character Acts	Character's Personality
John Thompson	"The Hatmaker's Sign"	man dressed in colonial clothing	listens to everyone's opinion	a follower not a decision maker
Merchant	"The Rich Man and the Shoemaker"			
Shoemaker	"The Rich Man and the Shoemaker"			
Colin Jenkins	"The Singing Hat"			
The Emperor	"The Emperor's New Clothes"			

Character Development
Self-Awareness

Self-awareness helps us choose between conflicting options.

Each person is an individual with his or her own thoughts, feelings, and opinions. Sometimes, people make personal decisions based on what others think, rather than thinking through a decision themselves. Make a chart to organize your thoughts when you have a decision to make. Use the chart to help clarify your options.

Technology
Make a Coat of Arms

Use the clip-art option in a word processing program to design a coat of arms that describes you. Use illustrations that represent you and your interests. Include at least four illustrations.

C

D

Erandi's Braids

by
Antonio
Hernández
Madrigal

Illustrated by
Tomie
dePaola

When they arrived at the lake, women and men from the village were already fishing. Erandi's mamá unfolded their net. "Look, Erandi, more holes. I won't be able to repair it any more. We need a new net so badly." Then she paused. "Soon we will have the money to buy one."

Erandi was surprised. They had so little money. Before she could ask Mamá where she would get the money, her friend Isabel ran up.

"*Buenos días*, Erandi. Can you come and play?" Isabel called.

"Go," Mamá said, "but come back and help me sort the fish."

Isabel and Erandi ran across the fields of flowers. "Are you going to the fiesta next Sunday?" Isabel asked.

The fiesta! Erandi remembered her birthday and the new dress she hoped to wear in the procession. But maybe Mamá needed the money for the new net instead. "I'm not sure," she said.

Throughout the day Erandi went back and forth, playing with Isabel and helping her mamá separate the small fish from the large fish. Then it was time to go. Erandi was afraid to ask about her birthday, and Mamá didn't say anything about it or the new net as they walked home.

But the next morning after making *tortillas*, Mamá said, "It's time to go to Señora Andrea's shop, Erandi." Erandi smiled. She knew she would have a new dress for the fiesta after all.

As they entered the shop in the square, Erandi saw a beautiful doll wearing a finely embroidered yellow dress up on the shelf.

Mamá saw Erandi stare at the doll.
"Erandi," Mamá said, "what do you want for your birthday?"

Erandi wanted the doll, but she knew she couldn't have both the doll and the dress. She pointed to a yellow dress, the same color as the doll's.

"Maybe next year we can buy you a doll," Mamá said as she paid for the dress.

After they left the shop, Mamá turned to Erandi and said, "Now we will go to the barber shop."

Erandi caught her breath. *My hair! So that is how Mamá is going to get the money for a new net. She is going to sell my braids.* Erandi shivered at the thought of the barber cutting off her braids. But she didn't say anything to Mamá.

They reached Miguel's Barber Shop and went inside. Erandi looked across the room crowded with women. She gripped Mamá's hand and huddled in her skirt. She didn't look at the barber chair, but she couldn't help hearing the sharp *snip snip* of scissors.

Will my hair ever grow back? she worried.

The line of women moved slowly, and Erandi's heart pounded as she and Mamá reached the front.

"Next person!" the barber called out.

Gazing at the enormous scissors in his hand, Erandi felt her knees tremble. But before she could move, Mamá walked to the chair and sat down.

I should have known Mamá would never sell my hair, Erandi thought as she watched the barber wrap a white apron around her mamá's shoulders and measure her hair.

"Your hair is not long enough," she heard the barber say.

Her mamá's face reddened with embarrassment. Without a word, she got out of the chair and took Erandi's hand. As they turned to leave, the barber noticed Erandi's braids. "Wait," he called out. "We will buy your daughter's hair."

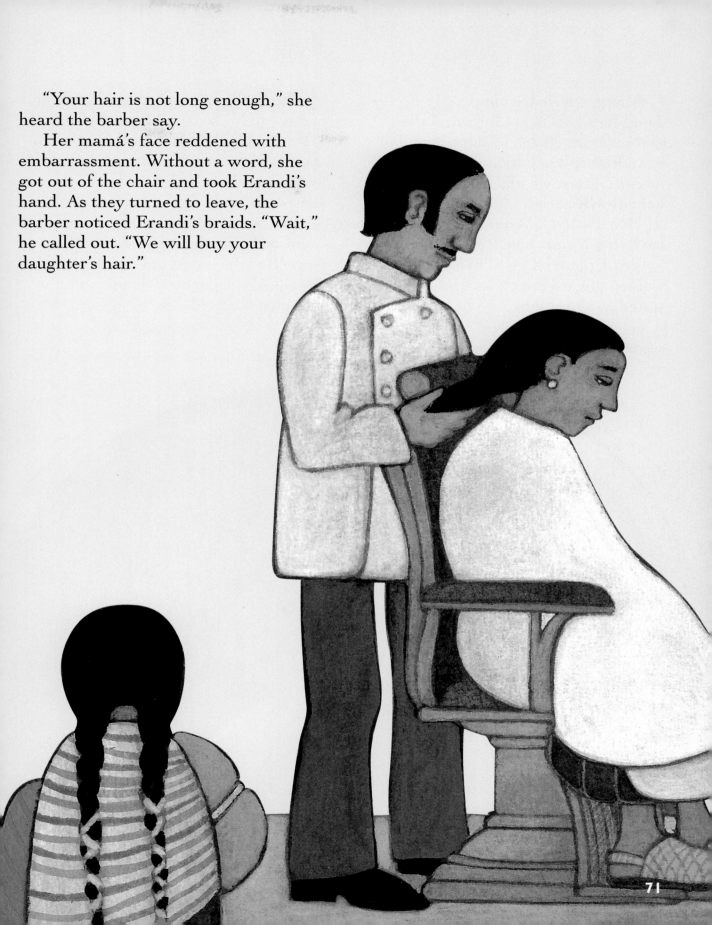

Mamá whirled around. "My daughter's hair is not for sale," she said proudly. Then she felt the pull of Erandi's hand and looked down.

"Sí, Mamá, we will sell my braids," Erandi whispered.

"No, *mi hija*," Mamá said. "You don't have to sell your hair."

But Erandi let go of her hand and walked toward the chair. The women stared as she climbed up onto the seat.

mi hija (mē ē′ hä) Spanish for "my daughter"

The barber measured her braids and picked up his scissors. Erandi closed her eyes. Her hands turned cold when she felt the metal scissors rub against her face and neck and she heard the sharp *snip snip*.

The barber moved to the second braid and Erandi's eyes filled with tears. But she dared not cry. Instead she asked the barber, "Señor, will my hair grow back?"

72

"Of course! It will grow just as long and pretty as before," he told her.

Erandi kept her eyes shut until the barber had finished. Then she opened them slowly and looked in the mirror. Her hair reached just below the bottom of her ears.

Out in the street, the air was cold on the back of her neck. How strange it felt without her hair. Mamá walked beside her, not saying a word. Only the hollow clapping of their *huaraches* broke the silence of the cobblestone streets.

Why didn't Mamá speak? Was she angry with her for cutting her hair? Or maybe the haircutter had not paid enough for her braids?

Finally Erandi peeked at her mamá's face and saw she was crying. "Forgive me, Erandi, I shouldn't have let you sell your hair," Mamá sobbed, wiping her face with an old handkerchief.

Now Erandi understood that her mamá was not angry with her. She had only been thinking of Erandi's hair. "Don't worry, Mamá. My braids will grow back as long and pretty as before."

huaraches (wə **rä′** chĕs) *n. pl.*
flat-heeled sandals with woven leather strips

Comprehension Check

Strategy: **Text-to-Self Connections**
Describe a time you had to give up something that was important to you.

Skill: **Analyze Characters' Motivations**
Why did Erandi's mother sit in the barber's chair before Erandi could?

SCIENTIFIC

by Sharon Franklin

Imagine This

Have you ever participated in a school science fair? Imagine entering your science project in an international contest and winning a Young Science Award and a $50,000 college scholarship! In 2006, three teenagers did just that.

Science is all about looking into the future. Scientists ask lots of questions. They wonder why things work, why they don't, or how they could. Then scientists test their ideas. These ideas shape our understanding of the universe.

Careers in science require hard work, education, and making priorities. If you think you have to be an adult to make a difference in the world of science, think again!

Fighting Infection

Inspired by her grandmother, 16-year-old Madhavi Gavini wondered how to prevent a deadly infection in patients with impaired immunity. Their immunity is weak because they are already fighting cancer, AIDS, or serious burns. Many people die each year from these infections. Madhavi found a new way to help them using an herb called Terminalia Chebula, a relative of the walnut that is commonly applied in traditional and alternative medicine.

Hannah Wolf, Madhavi Gavini, and Meredith MacGregor receive top honors at the 2006 Intel International Science and Engineering Fair in Indianapolis, Indiana.

GENRE

Narrative Nonfiction
- a piece of writing based on real people and events
- gives facts about an event
- written as a story and told in chronological order

MINDS

Mixed Nuts

If you told 17-year-old Meredith MacGregor that her idea was "nutty," you'd be right! Have you ever noticed how Brazil nuts always end up at the top of a can of mixed nuts? Meredith used this information to study what process forces large particles to the tops of containers and the smallest particles to the bottoms. Her findings provided new insight for pharmaceutical companies on how to combine all the particles in a drug evenly. Meredith's discovery has other applications, too. Her findings also interest scientists studying rockslides and other geologic events.

Try it!

You can duplicate Meredith MacGregor's experiment at home or in the classroom.
What you'll need:

- one jar with a lid
- small objects of varying sizes: pebbles, marbles, nuts, bolts, dried beans

Fill the jar with the objects, and shake it up. Note how the objects tend to move. Where are the smallest objects? Where are the largest objects? Repeat three times, noting how the objects move when they are shaken. Then repeat the experiment, this time rolling the jar on the floor. Are your results different?

Rock and Roll

Maybe 16-year-old Hannah Wolf likes to travel. Maybe she likes rocks. Maybe that's why she decided to study the rock formations in the Grand Staircase-Escalante National Monument. Long ago, earthquakes created these formations, which Wolf measured, photographed, charted, mapped, and analyzed. She wanted to find the earthquake's epicenter and learn how far, and in what direction, it moved. Her findings will eventually help scientists accurately predict and assess earthquake damage.

Science continues to advance as scientists around the world discover new things. But remember, unlike driving or riding a giant roller coaster, there is no minimum age or height requirement to study science! All you need to do is set your priorities, engage your curiosity, and have a strong desire to make a difference in the world.

Comprehension Check

Strategy: **Text-to-Self Connections**
What kinds of science experiments have you conducted?

Skill: **Points of View**
Choose one of the three teenagers from the selection. Describe what science means to her from her point of view.

The Moon Was at a Fiesta

by Matthew Gollub
Pictures by Leovigildo Martinez

GENRE

Fable

- a short tale that can be prose or poetry
- includes speaking animals or objects as characters
- teaches a lesson

For hundreds of years, the sun and the moon stayed in their separate skies. It was the sun's job to shine all day long while people went about their work.

It was the moon's job to watch over people's dreams.

Both were happy with this arrangement until the night moon overheard the stars gossip. Some stars wished they could come out with the sun. "All the games and feasts," they said, "take place under the sun's brilliant rays. And those are the times when people wear their most colorful clothes."

The moon imagined how lonely she would be if the stars really left her. So she tried to learn the sun's secret for fun by staying awake while the sun was out. But sooner or later she'd nod off to sleep.

Then one afternoon, a great commotion awakened her. Bleary eyed, she gazed down upon the earth. Fireworks mounted to toy animals spun and popped over people's heads.

Towering, stilt-legged *monigotes* were dancing round and round. The sun appeared to be enjoying himself immensely, laughing as he arched across the sky. The moon heard people call this celebration a fiesta.

It made the moon jealous to see so many people sing and parade about during the day. At night, they just slept so they could wake up early and start work in their fields. Never had she seen such merriment as this.

"I'll make my own fiesta," she decided aloud.

monigotes (mō nĕ gō′ tās) *n. pl.* Spanish for "paper dolls" or "rag dolls"

"You'd better not," warned the sun. "If you do, you'll fade and throw the world off balance."

Still, the moon wanted to please the restless stars, so that evening she gathered the watchmen who guarded the village at night.

"A nighttime fiesta would be magnificent!" they cried, for they too had to sleep during the day.

"Then for a fiesta," said the moon, "we'll need food and drink." She thought back on what she'd seen that afternoon. "And music," she added, "so that everyone can dance."

As other people came out of their homes to listen, the moon talked of ways to make *her* fiesta special.

"Why not have everyone bring lanterns?" clacked a *monigote*. The giant doll had stalked over, following a man who couldn't sleep.

"Lanterns at night look pretty," clattered another. This *monigote* pointed to a watchman's *farol,* and everyone agreed to bring paper lamps.

Next, the moon named *padrinos* to arrange for all the food. They hiked to a peaceful river bank where bulls, armadillos, boars, and iguanas came to drink the sweet water at night.

When the *padrinos* said they needed food for the fiesta, the animals agreed to help honor the moon.

Just then, a mermaid glided across the water. "I can bring shrimps and fish," she offered.

farol (fä rōl′) *n.* Spanish for "streetlamp"
padrinos (pä drē′ nōs) *n. pl.* Spanish for "godfathers" or "best men"

78

"Then by all means join us!" urged the hosts by the shore. The mermaid dove beneath the surface to search for tasty shellfish.

The *padrinos* decorated the site of the fiesta, and at last the awaited night arrived. The *mole,* tamales, and fish soups were ready.

People dressed in their most festive clothes and even wooden masks. Then everyone gathered amid the glow of lanterns and merrily began to eat, drink, and dance.

mole (mō′ lā′) *n.* a Mexican sauce made with chocolate, chilies, and spices

79

The moon remembered how the sun had laughed as he arched across the sky. Now, the moon felt just as pleased. She beamed on the gathering with lavish colors. The stars were so delighted they sparkled brighter than ever, and no one said a word about coming out with the sun.

The people below enjoyed themselves, too, particularly the men who offered the moon food and drink. The moon, who had never tasted food, liked the flavors so well she stayed high overhead. They gave her a little more. Then a little more.

But the more the moon ate and drank, the less she could give off light. And the less the moon could brighten the sky, the more the people lost track of time. Before she knew it, the sun was rising, and the moon had forgotten to go behind the sky!

She watched the sun shine as cheerfully as ever while the people dragged themselves home to sleep. Rather than watch over people's dreams, she'd kept them out all night!

The moon, by now reduced to a glimmer, could see what trouble she had caused. Corn was not ground that morning, fields were not plowed. Crops would have to be planted late and would not grow as tall.

For years, the remorseful moon stayed in her evening sky as before. But she never forgot the fun that she and the stars had that night. And to this day she likes to celebrate occasionally.

That's why in Oaxaca, when people rise with the sun and see the moon, they say, "The moon was at a fiesta."

Oaxaca (wə hä′ kə) *n.* a city in southeastern Mexico

80

Comprehension Check

Strategy: **Text-to-Self Connections**
In this story, the moon learns a lesson about making decisions that aren't good for everyone. Describe a lesson that you have learned this year.

Skill: **Identify Personification**
How is the moon like a person in this story?

81

GOHA
Gives His Son a Lesson About Life

Retold by Denys Johnson-Davies
Sewing by Hany El Saed Ahmed
From Drawings by
Hag Hamdy Mohamed Fattouh

GENRE

Folktale
- a story about real-life problems
- handed down through generations by word of mouth
- can include imaginary characters and events

Goha was a man who didn't worry about what other people might think about him. "Do what you believe is right," he would say, "and let people think what they like."

But Goha had a son who was always worrying about what people would say or think about him. Goha wanted to teach him a lesson.

So Goha saddled his donkey and asked his son to accompany him to the next village. With Goha riding the donkey and his son walking behind them, they passed by some men gathering at a coffee shop.

"Look at that selfish man who rides the donkey and makes his poor son walk," one man whispered to another.

So Goha got down from the donkey and told his son to get on. Goha would walk.

Now they passed by another gathering of people at a marketplace, who pointed at the boy. "Just look at the boy, letting his poor father walk. He has no manners and no respect for grown-ups."

82

So Goha climbed up behind his son, and they both rode the donkey.

"Poor donkey," some people standing near the road said, "and how unfair that he has to carry the man and the boy."

So Goha and his son carried the donkey between them. "Now, let's see what people have to say," Goha said.

Of course, now everyone laughed at them. "How ridiculous of that madman and his son, trying to carry the donkey instead of riding it!"

When the donkey was once again walking on its own four legs, Goha turned to his son and said, "You should know, my son, that in life, it is impossible to please everyone. So do not spend time worrying about what people think."

Street of the Tentmakers

In Cairo, Egypt, lies the Street of the Tentmakers. Men sit on platforms inside the one-room stores, sewing wall hangings, bedspreads, and table covers that cover the walls of their shops.

In one of these tiny stalls sit Hany and his uncle, Hag Hamdy, who illustrated this story.

Comprehension Check

Strategy: **Text-to-Self Connections**
Describe something you have learned from a parent or another adult.

Skill: **Analyze Character Relationships**
Describe what Goha thinks about his son.

LIFTOFF!

THE ELLEN OCHOA STORY

by Lisa Benjamin

In 1993, Ellen Ochoa gazed out a window to marvel at Earth a million miles away. Ochoa was an astronaut on a spaceship orbiting our planet. Ambition, setting priorities, and hard work enabled Ochoa to reach such great heights.

GENRE

Narrative Nonfiction

- a piece of writing based on real people and events
- gives facts about an event
- written as a story and told in chronological order

Setting Priorities

In 1993, Ellen Ochoa became the first Latina woman to soar into space. She was part of the *Discovery* shuttle crew, assigned to gather information from satellites to analyze Earth's climate and environment. "I never got tired of watching the Earth, day or night, as we passed over it," she recalled.

Becoming an astronaut isn't Ochoa's only achievement. She is also a scientist and an inventor. Plus, she flies airplanes, plays the flute, and loves volleyball and bicycling. She is married and has two children. It's not always easy to juggle all of her responsibilities. However, Ochoa learned a long time ago that the only way to make anything happen was to prioritize her goals and work toward them.

Ellen Ochoa at Vance Air Force Base, Houston, Texas

A space shuttle orbits Earth.

Dreaming Big

One of five children, Ochoa was ambitious even as a child. She wanted to accomplish something amazing one day. Her mother told her that with education and hard work, she could become anything she imagined. Ochoa quickly discovered that she didn't mind hard work. In school, she developed a love of math and science and earned excellent grades.

When Ochoa was 11 years old, astronaut Neil Armstrong walked on the moon for the first time. Although she wanted to do something extraordinary, Ochoa never imagined she might follow in his footsteps. At that time, no woman had completed astronaut training.

Instead, Ochoa, a talented flutist, thought of joining an orchestra after college. Remembering her mother's words about the value of education, Ochoa decided to attend graduate school for electrical engineering at Stanford University.

During Ochoa's time at Stanford, another pioneer, Sally Ride, became the first woman to travel into space. A new dream materialized—if Sally Ride could become an astronaut, maybe Ochoa could, too. She knew her graduate degree would be a tremendous advantage. After completing her education, she applied for the astronaut program at the National Aeronautics and Space Administration (NASA). Ochoa knew that she'd chosen a difficult path. NASA would have to be her top priority if she wanted to succeed.

Ochoa and the space shuttle crew head to the Astrovan to go to a simulated launch countdown.

Working Hard

Ellen Ochoa began her astronaut training in 1990 at the Johnson Space Center in Houston, Texas. The program was extremely demanding. To complete the program, she needed to succeed in a variety of subjects, including mechanics, medicine, and meteorology. She also learned parachuting and survival techniques. In time, Ochoa became an expert on the space shuttle, both as a scientist and as an engineer.

Ochoa officially completed her training in July 1991. Since then, she has flown several missions, performing tasks such as operating a robotic arm to retrieve satellites. "Being an astronaut allows you to learn continuously, like you do in school," Ochoa says. "One flight, you're working on atmospheric research. The next, it's . . . space station design."

Ochoa has never forgotten the importance of setting priorities. She often speaks to students about the astronaut program and shares the lessons she's learned in life—that hard work can make dreams come true.

Ochoa during training at Vance Air Force base, Houston, Texas, 1993

MISSIONS IN SPACE

Ochoa is currently Deputy Director of Flight Crew Operations. She has spent more than 978 hours in space performing various tasks.

1993: *(Discovery)* deployed and captured a satellite

1994: *(Atlantis)* studied Earth's atmosphere

1999: *(Discovery)* docked on the International Space Station and completed an 8-hour space walk

2002: *(Atlantis)* used a robotic arm to maneuver space walkers around the International Space Station

Comprehension Check

Strategy: **Text-to-Self Connections**
How do Ochoa's dreams and goals compare to your own dreams and goals?

Skill: **Text Features: Charts**
Look at the chart above. What did Ellen Ochoa do on her second *Discovery* mission?

React and Respond

Comprehension Check
Strategy: Text-to-Self Connections

When you pause while reading and ask, "What does this have to do with me?" you are trying to make a text-to-self connection. Text-to-self connections help you relate a text to your own experiences in a meaningful way.

1. "Erandi's Braids" recounts how Erandi allows the barber to cut off her hair for her mother. Describe a time someone did something nice for you.

2. "Scientific Minds" explains how three young women used science to investigate answers to questions about life. Describe a time when you conducted an investigation to find the answer to one of your curiosities.

3. "The Moon Was at a Fiesta" is one explanation why some mornings the moon is still visible in the sky. Why might an author try to explain this phenomenon with a story?

4. In "Goha Gives His Son a Lesson About Life," Goha teaches his son that there is no way you can please everyone. How does this lesson relate to your own life?

5. "Liftoff! The Ellen Ochoa Story" describes how Ochoa manages her time as an astronaut, parent, and spouse. How do you manage all of your responsibilities?

Compare Texts
Make a Two-Column Chart

A Two-Column Chart can help you organize your thoughts about texts, so you can compare them side by side. For example, look at the comparison between what Erandi wants in "Erandi's Braids" to what the moon wants in "The Moon Was at a Fiesta."

What Characters Want	
Erandi	**Moon**
• to go to a celebration • a new dress • to keep her long hair • a birthday present	• to keep the stars company • to learn from the sun • a fiesta • to enjoy the daytime

Now, think about what Ellen Ochoa and the scientists from "Scientific Minds" want. Put your ideas in a Two-Column Chart.

Character Development
Priorities

Setting priorities helps us make choices that are right for us.

Think about your interests and hobbies. How do you balance your schoolwork and the time you'd spend on your other interests? By setting priorities, you decide how you will spend and divide your time. For example, will you go to your friend's birthday party or will you play in a baseball game? Look at the list of activities below. Prioritize your tasks. Compare your list with that of a friend. You may find that you have different priorities!

- Doing homework
- Making your bed
- Practicing a sport
- Writing e-mail to friends

- Calling a relative
- Eating dinner with your family
- Reading a book
- Listening to music

Technology
Listing Priorities

Use your list of priorities to make an artistic word list. With a word processing program, you can change the color, size, and font of the text. Make a list of your priorities that clearly shows what is most important to you. Share your list with your family.

Teamwork helps us combine our strengths and talents to solve problems.

The Island-Below-the-Star

**Written and Illustrated by
James Rumford**

One night, Hōkū said, "See, my brothers, that bright star there? There's an island below that star. Let us sail to it."

And as he spoke, the star sparkled with adventure.

Hōkū's four brothers looked up at the star over their own island and saw how very far away the other star was. No one had ever gone so far before.

Little Manu was first to speak. "I will go with you, Hōkū."

The other brothers, including Hōkū, laughed. Such a dangerous trip was out of the question for such a little boy.

"You might get washed overboard," said Nā'ale.

"Or frightened by the thunder and lightning," said 'Ōpua.

"Or blown away by the wind," said Makani. "Besides, you only care about birds."

The next morning, Manu stood watching as his four brothers prepared for their great trip without him to the Island-below-the-Star.

Hōkū dried bananas, taro, and breadfruit in the hot sun, for they would need much food.

Nā'ale fashioned dozens of fishhooks and readied the harpoons, for they would live off the sea as well.

'Ōpua watched the clouds and gathered only the sweetest rainwater, for they would be thirsty on their long trip.

Makani repaired the sails, for they would need to catch even the tiniest breeze if they were ever to reach the Island-below-the-Star.

After several weeks, the canoe was seaworthy and the food and water were loaded on board. There was a great celebration for the four brothers.

Little Manu did not join in. No one noticed as he hid himself among the calabashes of food and baskets of coconuts.

The brothers left just before dawn.

It was sunset before they discovered little Manu.

"Let's toss him overboard and let him swim back," said Nāʻale.

"Let's throw him into the air and let the wind carry him home," said Makani.

Big ʻŌpua picked Manu up and held him over the side of the canoe.

"Hōkū!" cried Manu with his arms outstretched. "Hōkū!"

"All right! All right!" shouted ʻŌpua. "We were just kidding."

Hōkū began to laugh. "But you had better behave yourself," he told Manu.

Manu stood there, his head down.

"Make yourself useful," said Nāʻale. "We need fish."

Each day, as Manu sat with his fishing line, he was in awe of his brothers.

Hōkū used the sun, the moon, and the twinkling stars like a map to guide them.

When the clouds covered the heavenly map, they turned to Nāʻale, who kept the canoe on course as he felt the rhythms of the ocean waves.

ʻŌpua was always there watching the clouds.

And when he predicted storms, Makani was at hand, disentangling the knotted wind as they sailed north to the Island-below-the-Star.

Several weeks later, it was Makani who first noticed a strange rush of warm air. He scanned the horizon.

The waves began to grow in strength as they slapped against the hull. Nā'ale alerted the others.

A thin palm frond of a cloud appeared above the horizon. 'Ōpua prepared his brothers for the worst.

By evening, the sky that Hōkū depended on was roiling with clouds. The waves were mountains. The wind was a knife.

The brothers tied a safety rope to Manu.

For five days and nights they hung on for dear life as they rode out the storm.

At last, the wind died down. The sea was calm, but the sky was still hidden behind a gray blanket of clouds. The canoe had been blown far off course. The brothers were lost.

Manu undid the safety rope. He had not cried when the thunder crashed through the sky. He had not been washed overboard or carried off by the wind.

Suddenly Manu stood very still. He could feel something coming.

He looked up and saw, perhaps on its way to the Island-below-the-Star, a tiny speck of a bird.

Manu called to his brothers, "Look, brothers, a bird! A bird on its way to land!"

"Where?" they cried. It was so high that they could not see it.

"Tell me where it is, Manu," said Hōkū. "Tell me which way to go."

Manu pointed in the direction the bird was flying, and Hōkū turned the canoe.

The bird stayed with the brothers all through the day, and Manu, proud Manu, told Hōkū of the bird's every turn.

That night, when the skies finally cleared, they all saw that they were beneath their star.

But where was the island?

Nā'ale showed them the waves crashing into one another, as though pushed back by something big.

'Ōpua pointed to the moonlit clouds gathered in the north as though caught by a mountain.

Makani told them how the wind was swirling oddly, as though avoiding some huge shape.

No one slept.

Manu, now part of the team, spotted the first birds in the predawn light.

They were close—very close.

And then, at dawn, they saw the island. Its peaks towered above the waves and caught the first rays of the rising sun. The brothers shouted with joy and lifted Manu high on their shoulders.

At noon, they found a quiet bay for the canoe.

At sunset, they set foot on shore.

That night, they gave thanks for their safe journey as they stood directly below the bright star that had called to them.

Comprehension Check

Strategy: Take Perspectives
In this legend from Hawaii, what kind of attitude do the characters develop in order to find the island?

Skill: Text Structure: Beginning, Middle, and End
Summarize what happens at the beginning, middle, and end of the story.

Daisy's Garden

Written and Illustrated by
Mordicai Gerstein and
Susan Yard Harris

GENRE

Poetry

- a form of writing often broken into verses, lines, and stanzas
- uses imaginative language and sensory details
- may include rhyme, rhythm, alliteration, or shape

"IT'S APRIL!" says Daisy.
"The earth smells sweet,
like chocolate cake
beneath my feet.
The warm breeze tells me
spring has come.
Let's plant a
garden, everyone!"

"A garden that we
all can share—
groundhog, rabbit,
skunk, and bear.
Field mice, crickets,
squirrel, and deer—
grab a hoe!
You're welcome here!"

"How can I help?"
asks the horse.
"Would you plow?"
"I would, of course!"

"What can we do?"
ask the moles.
"You can dig
some little holes."

The mice say,
"Everyone agrees,
we're the ones
to sow the seeds.

"Except a few
we'll save to munch,
in case we need
some snacks, or lunch."

The plump clouds sigh
as they float by.
"Your garden looks
a little dry."
First comes lightning.
Thunder crashes!
Everyone runs as
rain patters and splashes.

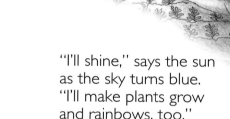

"I'll shine," says the sun
as the sky turns blue.
"I'll make plants grow
and rainbows, too."

"IT'S MAY," says the cat.
"I'll smile and purr
and watch sprouts grow
while I lick my fur."

"I'll bark," says the dog,
"and welcome crows."
The crows say, "Caw!
We'll thin the rows."

"Some sprouts," says Daisy,
"are really weeds.
Weeding is what
this garden needs."

"No! No!" says the goat.
"No need for weeding.
Weeds are tasty.
Just start eating!"

"IT'S JUNE! IT'S JUNE!"
sing the beetles and slugs.
"You can't have a garden
without us bugs."

"We'll fly," sing the swallows,
"from garden to nests,
stuffing our babies
with plump, tasty pests."
"Pest? Who's a pest?"
asks a cabbage moth's son.
"Isn't this garden
for everyone?"

"There are peas," cries Daisy,
"on every vine!"
"I'm a great peapicker,"
says a porcupine.

The rabbits say,
"Now don't forget us.
We can help you
pick the lettuce."
"Honeyhoneyhoney,"
hum the bees.
"We spread pollen
with our furry knees."

"IT'S JULY!" chirp the bluebirds.
"We will harvest the cherries."
"We," say the bears,
"will gather the berries."

"And look!" says Daisy.
"The tomatoes are ready!
Let's make a sauce.
We'll have spaghetti!"

"There are carrots, beets,
and bumpy cucumbers,
and I counted zucchini
till I ran out of numbers . . ."

"And peppers," says a lizard,
"and collard greens,
string, lima, kidney,
and pinto beans!"

"IN AUGUST," raccoons croon,
"call evening or morn.
We'll come in a hurry
and pick all the corn."

Says the pig, "I am proud
of my sensitive snout.
It sniffs the potatoes
and then digs them out."

"Like me," says the moon,
"the pumpkins are round.
I grow in the sky;
they grow on the ground.
By my gentle
silvery light,
shy visitors can
come at night.

"Some hop, some fly,
some nibble and run.
A garden is for everyone."

"SEPTEMBER!" cries Daisy.
"Come one and all
for a harvest picnic
to welcome fall.
What could be better,
as summer ends,
than feasting and dancing
with all our friends?

"Everything's ready,
ripe and sweet.
There's nothing to say,
except, 'Let's eat!'
And thank you, each,
for all you've done."
"Hooray for Daisy!"
says everyone.

"OCTOBER," sigh
the deer and crow.
They always are
the last to go,
sniffing the wind
for hints of snow.

Then Daisy hears
the wind's new song:
"Here comes winter,
cold and long."

And Daisy hears
the chickadee sing:
"Good-bye, garden,
until next spring!"

Strategy: Take Perspectives
What do all of the creatures in Daisy's
garden think about the garden?

Skill: Identify Sound Devices: Rhyme, Rhythm
Clap out the rhythm in this poem as you
read it again aloud.

PITCH BLACK

by Douglas L. Leiva

Genre

Narrative Nonfiction
- a piece of writing based on real people and events
- gives facts about an event
- written as a story and told in chronological order

Crowds gather outside Grand Central Station after the blackout in New York City, New York.

On any normal night, the lights of the East Coast can be seen easily from space. On August 14, 2003, those lights went out, leaving 50 million people in the United States and Canada in the dark.

The Lights Go Out

Just after 4 P.M., a power surge knocked out power in northeast Ohio. As circuits overloaded, the strain on surrounding power grids caused more power failures. Within minutes, the power was out in eight states and parts of Canada.

In New York City, people were beginning to leave work. The sun was still shining. Lisa, an attorney in New York City, remembers that day well. "The power went out in our office, and my coworkers and I immediately evacuated. When I got down to the street, I realized it wasn't just our building. My coworker and I hailed the only available cab to get to Grand Central to try to get home. That's when we realized it was the whole city!"

We're in This Together

In daylight, the lights weren't people's biggest concern. When the power failed altogether, however, thousands were trapped in elevators and subway cars. Others were in offices 80 floors above the ground and had to walk down thousands of stairs. Traffic lights went out, leaving cars clogging the streets. Millions who relied on trains to get home were stranded, and cell phone service quickly overloaded. How would they get home? How would they check on their loved ones?

Dealing With Disaster

In Manhattan, New York, people lined up at pay phones to talk to their families. Others listened to battery-powered radios to stay informed. As night fell, candles illuminated the way through the dark. Millions of people walked Manhattan's streets, and many helped each other. Firefighters rescued hundreds of people stuck in elevators. More than 40,000 police officers patrolled the streets to maintain the peace. Civilians helped direct traffic. Others became leaders among the thousands of commuters caught between stations and trapped in subways. Thousands ended up sleeping in Central Park or on the steps of public buildings, side by side with strangers.

Across the Northeast, authorities warned that water sanitation plants had lost power as well. People were urged to boil water before drinking it. In Michigan, the power outage closed the Detroit-Windsor Tunnel, which links Detroit and Canada. About 27,000 cars drive the tunnel daily. Massachusetts and Vermont were largely spared, as they were not connected to the grid that powers New York.

Commuters cross the Queensborough Bridge in New York City, New York, during the blackout.

DISASTER PLANS

Does your family have a disaster plan? If the power goes out where you live, you need to know what to do.

- **Disaster Kit:** Every home should have a portable container with emergency supplies in a safe place. Your kit should contain bottled water, canned food, flashlights, blankets, and a battery-powered radio.

- **Fire Plan:** In case of a fire, choose a place for your family to meet. It should be a place you know well, such as your neighbor's house or a nearby street corner. You may want to post your fire plan on your refrigerator or by your phone.

- **Evacuation Plan:** Ask your parents to select a place to meet if you cannot reach your home. Your evacuation site should be outside your neighborhood. A family friend's or relative's house is a good choice.

- **Emergency Contact:** With your parents, choose someone outside your state to check in with if you are separated from your family. Your contact can help you reconnect with your family during an emergency. You should carry your contact's name and phone number with you at all times.

The Lights Come Back On

Over the next several days, engineers worked around the clock to restore service throughout the Northeast. By late Friday, Pennsylvania, New Jersey, Connecticut, and New York had power. Ohio's power came back Saturday, with Michigan following on Sunday. People continued to help one another, this time by conserving power. During the entire blackout, only eight people died as a direct result of the power failure. Millions of others experienced the power of teamwork firsthand.

This blackout ranks as the greatest energy disaster in the history of the United States. Yet, authorities and civilians teamed up to help each other. Strangers walked home together across New York's mighty bridges. Others simply looked to the sky and marveled at the sight of the Milky Way, which was clearly visible in city skies for the first time in decades. Through it all, people worked together—even if it was in the dark!

Comprehension Check

Strategy: **Take Perspectives**
What might it have been like to be stranded miles from home during the blackout?

Skill: **Describe a Setting**
Use your five senses to describe a time the lights went out at school or home. How did you get through the situation?

Working and Playing Together

by Stephen Currie

Making Peace

One great way to settle a quarrel is to talk to the person who's bothering you. You've probably settled plenty of arguments just this way. Seeking help from an adult can be a smart idea, too, especially if the situation is more than you can handle on your own.

For some arguments, though, the best choice may be peer mediation. A peer is a person like you, and *mediation* means "helping to settle a quarrel." In peer mediation, a group of students hears both sides of an argument. Then, the group helps find a solution everyone can agree on.

How Peer Mediation Works

Let's look at an example. Amber and Mimi had been best friends for years, so it was a surprise when they had a huge argument before science class one morning. By the time class started, Mimi was in tears, and Amber wouldn't even look at her friend.

Ms. Rodriguez, the principal, hoped that the girls would make peace on their own. But after a day or two, it was obvious that Amber and Mimi needed help to settle their problem. Ms. Rodriguez called the school's peer mediators together. She asked them to meet with Mimi and Amber, and she asked one of the mediators, Kimiko, to run the meeting.

The Rules

Kimiko started the meeting by outlining the rules. She explained that Mimi and Amber would each have a turn to speak. She reminded them both to listen to each other and to treat one another with respect. Then she invited Mimi to start.

Mimi began by describing how frustrated she had been feeling with Amber. "She only wants to spend time with Claire," she said. "She never wants to be with me!" On the day of the argument, Mimi said, she had invited Amber to come to her house after school. She added that Amber had balked, saying: "Who'd want to hang out with you?"

Amber's Turn

Amber admitted that she might have been rude to Mimi, but she had been feeling frustrated, too. "Mimi and I used to be best friends," she said, "but we have less in common now. Besides, Mimi doesn't like Claire. When I suggest that all three of us do something together, Mimi says no. I shouldn't have to choose between my friends!"

After both Mimi and Amber had spoken, Kimiko thanked them for talking honestly about their feelings and for not interrupting each other. Then the mediators asked a few questions. For instance, Peter asked Amber if she could have responded to Mimi's invitation in another way. Miguel asked why Mimi didn't like Claire. Kimiko wondered what interests Amber and Mimi still had in common.

Agreements

As they thought about the mediators' queries, the two girls became less angry and better able to see each other's point of view. By the end of the session, they had come to an agreement. Amber promised to spend some of her lunch periods just with Mimi, and Mimi promised to try to make friends with Claire. Both girls also apologized to each other for the argument.

Maybe Mimi and Amber might never be as close as they once were, Kimiko thought as she stood up to leave, *but that was all right.* With the help of peer mediation, the two friends had made peace. Kimiko was proud that peer mediation had been able to help.

Comprehension Check

Strategy: **Take Perspectives**
Why was Mimi frustrated with Amber?

Skill: **Note Details**
What were the different steps the peer mediators took to resolve the conflict? Why is each step important?

Step by Step: Peer Mediation

1. Two or more students have a conflict or an argument.

2. An adult suggests peer mediation, or the students ask for it on their own.

3. The peer mediators meet with the students who are arguing.

4. Each student has a turn to talk without interruption while everyone in the room listens.

5. The peer mediators can ask questions or make suggestions. The students might have ideas of their own.

6. The mediators help the arguing students make a plan to get along. The plan must be acceptable to both students, even if they have to compromise.

THE HOTTEST THING ON ICE

by Peter Gutiérrez

Jamaica is famous for its beautiful beaches and year-round warm temperatures. Since 1988, however, it has become known for something else—bobsledding!

Blazing an Icy Trail

In 1987, army lieutenant Devon Harris saw an intriguing notice in an army publication. It called for volunteers to "undergo rigorous and dangerous training." As a runner, he was interested because he wanted to represent his tropical Jamaica in the 1988 Olympics. However, there was a catch—the training was for the winter games.

Expository Nonfiction
- a factual piece of writing
- focuses on real people, places, and events
- describes, informs, explains, or persuades

At first, no one wanted to join the bobsledding team. Team organizers George Fitch and William Maloney then pitched their idea to the army. Jamaica's sprinters would make ideal "pushers," the people who pushed the bobsled at the top of the course.

It was already autumn when Devon Harris saw the advertisement. Tryouts were held in September, and the final team was to be in place by early January. Harris was joined by Dudley Stokes, Michael White, and Caswell Allen. Stokes and White were also military veterans, and Allen was a student.

Qualifying for the Olympics

The team members' backgrounds provided the discipline and cooperation these beginners needed. The team was poorly financed and lacked the equipment and facilities that other countries had. Teamwork was crucial—it was one of the few things that the team did have going for it. Soon, to the shock of many, the Jamaicans qualified for the Olympics.

Pushing Into History

The team had already arrived in Calgary, Canada, for the games when Allen fell during a training run. Stokes called his brother Chris, a sprinter, and invited him to join the team at the Olympics. Although the event was scheduled for the coming weekend, everyone helped Chris learn the new sport—in three days!

In the seventh heat of the competition, Chris Stokes's explosive speed gave the Jamaicans the fourth-fastest start time of any country. Unfortunately, the team's overall inexperience led to a terrifying crash in that same run.

Still, in the following years, the team improved. At the 1994 Olympics in Lillehammer, Norway, the team finished ahead of the United States. Winning medals at later competitions, the Jamaican Bobsled Team has inspired other tropical nations, including Mexico, and well deserves its slogan— "The Hottest Thing on Ice."

BOBSLEDDING TEAM

In a bobsledding race, each team member's role is crucial. The winning sled often beats the others by only hundredths of a second, so the team members must work together smoothly and efficiently to win.

PUSHERS

In a four-member team, two "pushers" start the race from outside the sled. The pushers must sprint while heaving the sled (and the other two members inside it) forward. After running for about 50 meters, the pushers jump into the sled just before the first turn.

DRIVERS

Each team has one driver. The driver sits at the front position and steers the sled. During turns, the driver tries to keep the sled low. If the sled skids too high up the walls, the team loses precious seconds.

BRAKEMEN

The brakeman sits at the rear of the sled and operates the brake. Once the sled reaches the finish, the brakeman pulls the brake upward to stop it.

Comprehension Check

Strategy: **Take Perspectives**
What were some reasons the members joined the bobsledding team?

Skill: **Make Generalizations**
Why is teamwork crucial in bobsledding?

React and Respond

Comprehension Check
Strategy: Take Perspectives

You may have heard the expression, "Walk a mile in someone else's shoes." The expression means to consider how someone else may view an issue or situation. As you read, try to consider how a character would react to the issues or events in the selection and how that reaction might differ from your own.

1. In "The Island-Below-the-Star," five brothers set out to find a new island. What do you think Manu thinks when he learns he is not included in the plans for the journey? Why do you think he sneaks onto the canoe?

2. "Daisy's Garden" shows how animals, people, and weather work together to keep a garden going. What might Daisy think about all of the help she receives when she gardens?

3. "Pitch Black" describes what it was like for people during the blackout in 2003. How do you think people reacted when they learned the entire region had no power?

4. "Working and Playing Together" tells about a problem-solving technique called peer mediation. Why should everyone listen to others' perspectives?

5. "The Hottest Thing on Ice" is about the development of a bobsled team in Jamaica. Why might an athlete from Jamaica be hesitant to start training for the winter Olympic games?

Compare Texts
Make a Venn Diagram

There are many different kinds of teams, but one thing teams have in common is that everyone is working toward a common goal. The Venn Diagram compares two types of teams: the bobsled team in "The Hottest Thing on Ice" and the brothers in "The Island-Below-the-Star."

Different Types of Teams

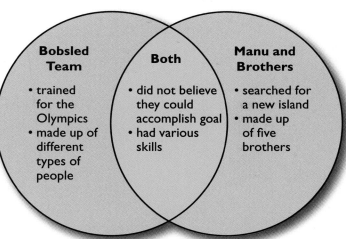

Bobsled Team
- trained for the Olympics
- made up of different types of people

Both
- did not believe they could accomplish goal
- had various skills

Manu and Brothers
- searched for a new island
- made up of five brothers

Character Development
Teamwork

Teamwork helps us combine our strengths and talents to solve problems.

People often work together as a team to solve problems. Different team members have different strengths that, when used together, can contribute to success for the whole group.

Try the following activity with your classmates. In groups of six or eight people, form a circle and face each other. Then close your eyes and reach out for a hand to grab. You will open your eyes and find yourself holding two different students' hands. Your task is to untangle, as a group, without letting go of anyone's hand. As you will see, you need to work as a team to untangle everyone!

Technology
Create an Acrostic Poem

Use a word processing program to make an acrostic poem. First, type the word *TEAMWORK* down the left side of the page. Then, come up with a word or phrase relating to teamwork that starts with each letter in the word *teamwork*. See the example for TEAM below. Use different font sizes and colors to make your poem look appealing. Share your poem with your classmates.

Together, we
Enable ourselves to
Achieve much
More than we could alone.

We respect people with integrity because they make choices that are fair to all.

The Legend of Bluebonnet

Retold by Judy Veramendi

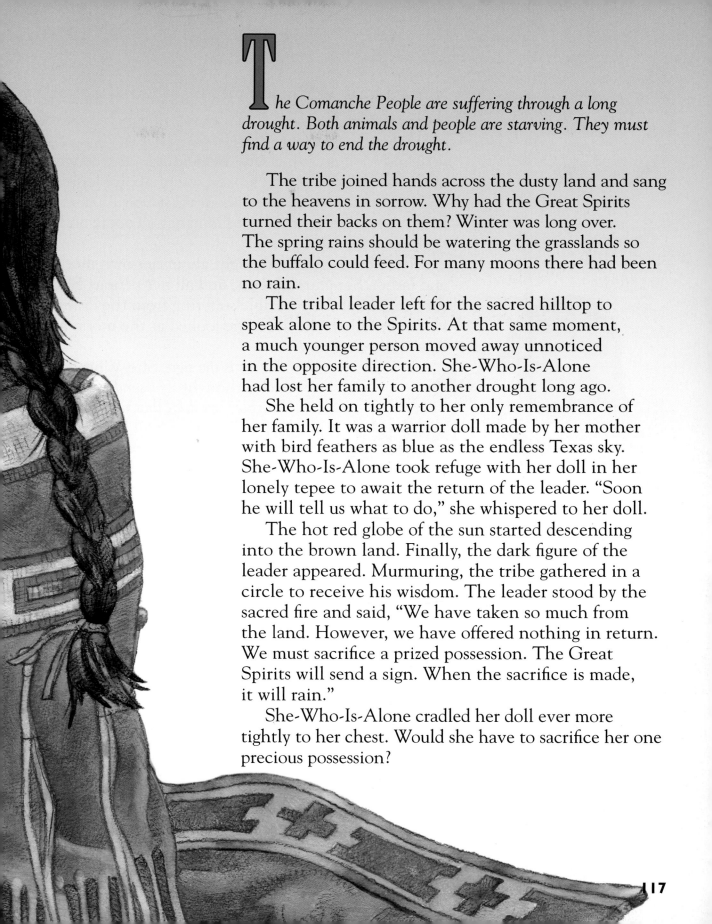

The Comanche People are suffering through a long drought. Both animals and people are starving. They must find a way to end the drought.

The tribe joined hands across the dusty land and sang to the heavens in sorrow. Why had the Great Spirits turned their backs on them? Winter was long over. The spring rains should be watering the grasslands so the buffalo could feed. For many moons there had been no rain.

The tribal leader left for the sacred hilltop to speak alone to the Spirits. At that same moment, a much younger person moved away unnoticed in the opposite direction. She-Who-Is-Alone had lost her family to another drought long ago.

She held on tightly to her only remembrance of her family. It was a warrior doll made by her mother with bird feathers as blue as the endless Texas sky. She-Who-Is-Alone took refuge with her doll in her lonely tepee to await the return of the leader. "Soon he will tell us what to do," she whispered to her doll.

The hot red globe of the sun started descending into the brown land. Finally, the dark figure of the leader appeared. Murmuring, the tribe gathered in a circle to receive his wisdom. The leader stood by the sacred fire and said, "We have taken so much from the land. However, we have offered nothing in return. We must sacrifice a prized possession. The Great Spirits will send a sign. When the sacrifice is made, it will rain."

She-Who-Is-Alone cradled her doll ever more tightly to her chest. Would she have to sacrifice her one precious possession?

After darkness fell, the young girl crept to the edge of the sacred circle. The full moon was glowing above. She startled and gazed more closely. Was that the face of a little girl looking at her sadly? Could it be the daughter of the Great Spirits? She looked so unhappy. Her mother and father must be worried about their Spirit Daughter. Is that why they ignored the Comanche People and their need for rain?

She-Who-Is-Alone thought about her own mother and father, her grandparents, and all her people. She thought about their terrible suffering from the drought. Her tears fell on the doll. She looked at the moon again. Was she crying too?

This is the sign, She-Who-Is-Alone thought. *If I send the Spirit Daughter my doll, that will make her happy. Then the Great Spirits will be happy, and we will have rain.*

She carried her doll to the leader, who gently placed it in the fire. As it burned, she watched the smoke and ashes ascend toward the spirits in the moon.

When only ashes remained, She-Who-Is-Alone scattered them to the four winds.

She-Who-Is-Alone lay down by the edge of the circle and fell asleep. In her dream, she heard her people singing songs of thanksgiving. When she awoke, she saw them standing about her. They were smiling in the soft morning mist.

"The Spirit Daughter has been crying with me and my doll. These are her tears," she told the leader. He helped her to her feet.

The circle of her people dispersed. She-Who-Is-Alone gasped with wonder. The hills were carpeted with bluebonnet flowers! They were as blue as the feathers on her doll.

A soft, steady rain began to fall. The leader said, "She-Who-Is-Alone received the sign and sacrificed her only beloved possession. She is no longer alone. She needs a new name. Now we will call her One-Who-Dearly-Loved-Her-People. Now our people will treasure her memory throughout time."

Each spring, the Great Spirits remember the young girl's sacrifice and scatter bluebonnets throughout the Texas hills, like blue stars in the grass.

Comprehension Check

Strategy: **Text-to-Text Connections**
Describe a hero from another story you have read.

Skill: **Understand Symbolism**
What do the bluebonnets in the story represent?

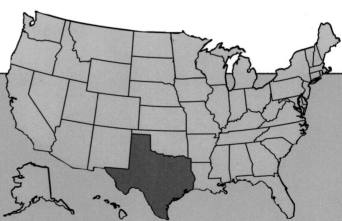

Texas State Flower: The Bluebonnet

The bluebonnet is a lupin. Its scientific name is *Lupinus texensis*. The small, spiky blue flower with silvery green leaves has other names as well. Some people call it buffalo clover or wolf flower. Others call it *el conejo* (ĕl kō **nā′** hō), which means "bunny" or "rabbit" in Spanish.

The Apple King

by Francesca Bosca
Illustrated by Giuliano Ferri
Translated by J. Alison James

The Apple King allows no one to visit his Royal Apple Tree but him. The tree grows lonely and invites worms to visit her, an act that first outrages the king and then teaches him a lesson.

The king was furious. "Enough!" he roared. "I will show these fiends who is in charge here!" He marched the entire royal army up to the tree, and within minutes they had the worms surrounded.

"Kill them, kill them all!" commanded the king. "But woe on you if you injure a single apple or harm my precious tree!"

Now, this was quite impossible. Every worm was in an apple, and every apple was on the tree. The royal army was forced to make a humiliating retreat.

The worms laughed and kept munching away on the sweet apples.

The king was beside himself. He sent out a proclamation declaring a reward of a sack of gold to anyone who could make the worms disappear.

A sly fox had his assistant climb the tree and cover up all the worm holes with thick red paint. Then they called the king. "Finished," they said. "There is not a worm to be seen."

The king was overjoyed. The sly fox and his accomplice disappeared with the sack of gold, and the king climbed up the tree to pick some apples. His mouth was already watering as he rushed back to the castle with a bowl filled with the luscious fruit.

But no sooner had the king taken a bite from the first apple when a worm crawled out and climbed on his nose.

"NOOOO!" bellowed the king. "What right do you wretched worms have to invade *my* apples?"

"But . . . but . . . but . . . we were invited!" said one of the apple worms.

"Invited! *Who* could have invited *you?*" shrieked the king.

"Why, the Royal Apple Tree invited us," explained the worm.

"You see, year after year she bears beautiful apples for nobody but you. No butterfly and no bird may visit her. No child may climb in her branches and take a sweet apple. The poor apple tree was terribly sad and lonely. Finally she invited us since we were small enough to sneak past the guard. At last she was happy that others could appreciate her fruit."

"What about *me?*" the king asked angrily. "I love my precious apple tree, and I adore my royal apples!"

"Do you think so?" asked the worm. "Are you sure you really care about what's best for the Royal Apple Tree?"

The king was hurt. How dare a worm speak to him this way? The entire royal household was staring at the worm in stunned surprise.

But what came next shocked them all. The king laughed!

"She is a remarkable tree," he declared. "And I will show her how much we all appreciate her. Everyone here will go out now and pick her beautiful apples. And this evening we will hold a Royal Apple Festival, with Apple Cider and Royal Apple Cake for all!"

Hearing this, the worms gladly abandoned the apples and crept off to get ready for the Festival.

It was a most splendid Apple Festival! The king had never felt more proud than when everyone praised the wonderful taste of his apples. And the people were proud of their king, whose generosity was as sweet as his apples!

From that day forward, each year at harvest time, the Royal Apple Festival was celebrated at the castle. The rich and powerful king had discovered that the royal apples tasted even more delicious when shared with cheerful company. And if the occasional apple worm was seen among the guests, the king was not bothered in the least.

Comprehension Check

Strategy: **Text-to-Text Connections**
How is the relationship of the worm and the Apple King similar to the relationships between characters in other stories you have read?

Skill: **Problem and Solution**
Why are the worms a problem for the king?

LOU
Gehrig:
The Luckiest Man

by David A. Adler
Illustrated by
Terry Widener

Lou Gehrig played despite stomachaches, fevers, a sore arm, back pains, and broken fingers. Lou's constant play earned him the nickname Iron Horse. All he would say about his amazing record was, "That's the way I am."

Lou was shy and modest, but people who watched him knew just how good he was. In 1927 Lou's teammate Babe Ruth hit sixty home runs, the most hit up to that time in one season. But it was Lou Gehrig who was selected that year by the baseball writers as the American League's Most Valuable Player. He was selected again as the league's MVP in 1936.

Then, during the 1938 baseball season—and for no apparent reason—Lou Gehrig stopped hitting. One newspaper reported that Lou was swinging as hard as he could, but when he hit the ball it didn't go anywhere.

Lou exercised. He took extra batting practice. He even tried changing the way he stood and held his bat. He worked hard during the winter of 1938 and watched his diet.

But the following spring Lou's playing was worse. Time after time he swung at the ball and missed. He had trouble fielding. And he even had problems off the field. In the clubhouse he fell down while he was getting dressed.

Some people said Yankee manager Joe McCarthy should take Lou out of the lineup. But McCarthy refused. He had great respect for Lou and said, "Gehrig plays as long as he wants to play." But Lou wasn't selfish. On May 2, 1939, he told Joe McCarthy, "I'm benching myself . . . for the good of the team."

When reporters asked why he took himself out, Lou didn't say he felt weak or how hard it was for him to run. Lou made no excuses. He just said that he couldn't hit and he couldn't field.

On June 13, 1939, Lou went to the Mayo Clinic in Rochester, Minnesota, to be examined by specialists. On June 19, his thirty-sixth birthday, they told Lou's wife, Eleanor, what was wrong. He was suffering from amyotrophic lateral sclerosis, a deadly disease that affects the central nervous system.

Lou stayed with the team, but he didn't play. He was losing weight. His hair was turning gray. He didn't have to be told he was dying. He knew it. "I don't have long to go," he told a teammate.

Lou loved going to the games, being in the clubhouse, and sitting with his teammates. Before each game Lou brought the Yankee lineup card to the umpire at home plate. A teammate or coach walked with him, to make sure he didn't fall. Whenever Lou came onto the field the fans stood up and cheered for brave Lou Gehrig.

But Yankee fans and the team wanted to do more. They wanted Lou to know how deeply they felt about him. So they made July 4, 1939, Lou Gehrig Appreciation Day at Yankee Stadium.

Many of the players from the 1927 Yankees—perhaps the best baseball team ever—came to honor their former teammate. There was a marching band and gifts. Many people spoke, too. Fiorello La Guardia, the mayor of New York City, told Lou, "You are the greatest prototype of good sportsmanship and citizenship."

When the time came for Lou to thank everyone, he was too moved to speak. But the fans wanted to hear him and chanted, "We want Gehrig! We want Gehrig!"

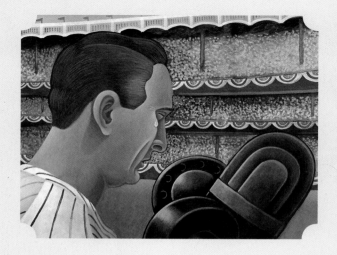

Dressed in his Yankee uniform, Lou Gehrig walked slowly to the array of microphones. He wiped his eyes, and with his baseball cap in his hands, his head down, he slowly spoke.

"Fans," he said, "for the past two weeks you have been reading about a bad break I got. Yet today I consider myself the luckiest man on the face of the earth."

It was a courageous speech. Lou didn't complain about his terrible illness. Instead he spoke of his many blessings and of the future. "Sure, I'm lucky," he said when he spoke of his years in baseball. "Sure, I'm lucky," he said again when he spoke of his fans and family.

Lou spoke about how good people had been to him. He praised his teammates. He thanked his parents and his wife, whom he called a tower of strength.

The more than sixty thousand fans in Yankee Stadium stood to honor Lou Gehrig. His last words to them—and to the many thousands more sitting by their radios and listening—were, "So I close in saying that I might have had a bad break, but I have an awful lot to live for. Thank you."

Lou stepped back from the microphones and wiped his eyes. The stadium crowd let out a tremendous roar, and Babe Ruth did what many people must have wanted to do that day. He threw his arms around Lou Gehrig and gave him a great warm hug.

The band played the song "I Love You Truly," and the fans chanted, "We love you, Lou."

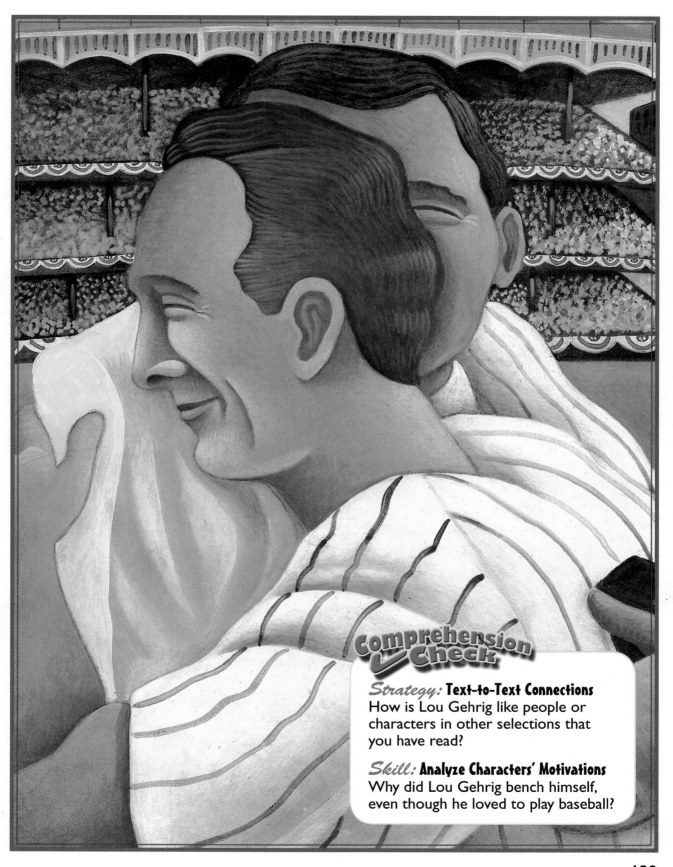

Comprehension Check

Strategy: Text-to-Text Connections
How is Lou Gehrig like people or characters in other selections that you have read?

Skill: Analyze Characters' Motivations
Why did Lou Gehrig bench himself, even though he loved to play baseball?

Queen Liliuokalani's Decision

by Jeri S. Cipriano

**Queen Liliuokalani abdicated
her throne so her people
could live in peace.**

GENRE

Biography
- a written account of someone's life
- told from the third-person point of view
- gives factual information about the person's life

Queen
Liliuokalani
circa 1898

Lydia Dominis Becomes Queen

Lydia Dominis was 52 years old when her brother died in 1891. Suddenly, Dominis became the queen of the Hawaiian Islands. The new queen inherited a kingdom in great unrest. During her brother's rule, sugar planters and investors in the United States had pressured the king to agree to a new constitution that reduced the powers of the kingdom. Liliuokalani hoped to restore and protect her royal authority and the political power of native Hawaiians.

At this time, Hawaiians were debating whether to join the United States. The queen was not in favor of joining. Liliuokalani wanted to protect her country from U.S. business interests, so she wanted to remain independent. She wanted a constitution that would not permit foreigners to vote, yet it never came to be. Powerful businesspeople in Hawaii had other ideas.

Liliuokalani (lē lē′ ठō ō kä lä′ nē)

131

The Last Queen of Hawaii

The Political Takeover

The Hawaiian Supreme Court upheld the queen's right to establish a new constitution. Nevertheless, some on the island wanted to be rid of the queen. They favored Hawaii's annexation to the United States. Sanford Dole, a powerful pineapple businessman, attempted to overthrow the queen. He had the support of U.S. Minister John Stevens and the help of a division of U.S. troops. Dole took the kingdom by force and established a temporary government in 1893.

Colonists from the United States had taken matters into their own hands. Not only did the colonists control most of Hawaii's economy, but now they had overthrown the government. Led by Sanford Dole, the colonists applied for annexation to the United States.

Queen Liliuokalani appealed to President Cleveland and asked to be reinstated to her rightful throne. President Cleveland sent a diplomat to investigate the situation. Indeed, the diplomat concluded, the colonists did not have the authority to depose the queen. U.S. Minister Stevens, too, had overstepped his power in recognizing Dole's new government.

Dole submitted a treaty, or official agreement, of annexation to the U.S. Senate. Some senators opposed it, especially after learning that most nat Hawaiians did not want annexation. President Cleveland sent a new U.S. minister to Hawaii to restore Queen Liliuokalani to the throne, bu Sanford Dole ignored the president's orders. D refused to step down as leader of the governm Hawaiians loyal to the queen revolted, but Dole forces proved stronger. Then Dole had many of Liliuokalani's supporters arrested.

Sacrifice for the Greater Good

President Cleveland's next minister offered to restore the queen to her throne. There was one condition: She would have to grant amnesty to those who had dethroned her. At first, the queen refused. Then she reconsidered, and the minister demanded that the government reinstate her. The government refused, reestablishing the Republic of Hawaii on July 4, 1894. Six months later, Liliuokalani was arrested and forced to abdicate, or give up, all claims to the throne in return for the release of her jailed supporters.

Queen Liliuokalani may have lost the throne, but she acted in the best interests of her subjects when she gave up her position. "I yield to the superior force of the United States," she explained. "To avoid any collision of armed forces and perhaps loss of life."

In 1898, the United States formally annexed the Hawaiian Islands. The queen was released as a private citizen and lived in Honolulu until her death in 1917. Her estate cares for orphans and poor children of the Hawaiian Islands. The Children's Center she established continues today. The people of Hawaii will not forget their queen's kind deeds and her selfless decision to put peace and their well-being above personal gain.

Comprehension Check

Strategy: Text-to-Text Connections

How is Queen Liliuokalani's decision similar to other decisions you have read about this year?

Skill: Fact and Opinion

Identify two facts and two opinions in the selection. How do you know they are facts or opinions?

Aloha 'Oe

Liliuokalani was an accomplished musician and composer. She wrote the song "Aloha 'Oe" in 1878.

*Proudly swept the rain by
    the cliffs
As it glided through the trees
Still following ever the bud
The 'ahihi lehua of the vale*

Chorus:

*Farewell to thee, farewell
    to thee
The charming one who dwells
    in the shaded bowers
One fond embrace,
'Ere I depart
Until we meet again*

*Sweet memories come back
    to me
Bringing fresh remembrances
Of the past
Dearest one, yes, you are
    mine own
From you, true love shall
    never depart*

*I have seen and watched
    your loveliness
The sweet rose of Maunawili
And 'tis there the birds of
    love dwell
And sip the honey
    from your lips*

Aloha 'Oe
(ä lō′ hä   ō′ wə)

Saving the Land

The United States is often considered the land of plenty. As natural resources run out, who will protect the bounty for future generations?

by
Nora Davis Day

From his window on East 20th Street in New York City, young Theodore Roosevelt had a view of the world that stretched far beyond the sights and sounds of the streets below. In his youth he had often been ill, but he loved the great outdoors. When he became the 26th president of the United States, Roosevelt fought to save the land he loved so much. Thanks to him, the "spacious skies and amber waves of grain" of a beautiful United States are still here for us to enjoy.

Even as a student, Roosevelt wrote about his fascination with animals, birds, and insects. He saw with his own eyes the huge flocks of passenger pigeons that darkened the skies in autumn. He remembered the herds of bison that once roamed the Texas plains.

Although he was born to a life of wealth and luxury, Roosevelt chose to focus on more than his own future. He chose a life of public service. While he served as president, Roosevelt exercised his power to remind the nation that the land's resources belong to the people. Saving the natural land is up to all of us.

Preserve, Conserve, or Develop?

Roosevelt's love of the outdoors brought him face to face with others who appreciated the wilderness. He learned much about natural resources from John Burroughs and John Muir. Burroughs was a noted naturalist and essayist. Muir wrote many essays and books about his adventures in the Sierra Nevada of California, especially Yosemite. Both men spent time in the wilderness with Roosevelt. They shared with him a strong belief in preserving the land for everyone to enjoy.

Vernal Falls at Yosemite National Park, California

Preserved Lands

There are 58 national parks, and more than 300 national monuments, trails, and other protected areas in the United States. Some of the most popular parks to visit include:

- Yellowstone in Wyoming and Montana
- Carlsbad Caverns, New Mexico
- The Everglades, Florida
- Denali, Alaska
- Grand Canyon, Arizona
- Great Smoky Mountains in Tennessee and North Carolina
- Acadia, Maine

Federal Preserved Lands in the United States

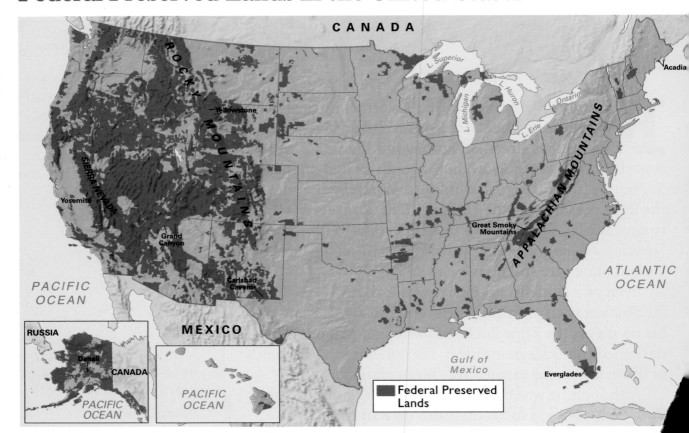

However, many did not agree with this perspective. Politicians and businesspeople debated furiously about what was best for the United States. Muir and Burrough wanted the government to set aside areas of land so that everyone could enjoy the beauty. These supporters were called preservationists. Others, including Gifford Pinchot, the first chief of the United States Forest Servi wanted the government to manage resources wisely— making some available for public use and some for commercial use. People who supported this idea w called conservationists. There were also those wh thought that the government should stay out of i allow private use of all public land. They were dev

In the end, Congress sided with the developers, not before President Roosevelt signed over 16 milli acres of forest land to the public. By the end of his t he had placed more than 200 million acres in public hands forever!

The Debate Continues

Maybe you've been to national parks, such as the Grand Canyon, Arizona; Yosemite, California; or Yellowstone, in Montana and Wyoming. Perhaps you have spent a slow afternoon biking through Central Park in New York City or riding down the Oregon coast—or even visited a local zoo, botanical garden, or beach. Each acre of that land is the result of years of protection and care.

Theodore Roosevelt is gone, and the view from his childhood window is certainly different—but the debate over just how to save the natural land still echoes in the halls of Congress. The language is new. Words like *ecology* and *environment* have been added to the list. Yet, the question is still the same: What should we do with our natural resources?

As the population grows, so does the need for resources. Where will they come from? Today, the question is much bigger than what to do with our forests and our farms. Now we must also decide what to do about pollution and energy. How will we conserve sea life and prevent global warming? Who will make the choices that are fair to all of us?

Comprehension Check

Strategy: **Text-to-Text Connections**
How does this article compare with "John Muir and Stickeen" in Week 1?

Skill: **Draw Conclusions**
What will happen if we don't continue to conserve and preserve natural resources?

Today's Environmentalists

You don't have to be a world leader to protect the environment. These students have all made a difference.

Gabriella, 16, from Puerto Rico: She was concerned about the local bird population, so she produced a 60-page pamphlet to educate others about local birds and how people can help protect the birds' habitat.

James, 14, from New York: He realized that local birds had few places to nest, and began building bird boxes for them. He still maintains the boxes and speaks out about saving animals.

Savannah, 13, from Florida: She began looking for ways to conserve oil to protect the natural beauty of Alaska. She started an organization to remind drivers to keep their tires properly inflated. Just doing this saves 4,000,000 gallons of gas every day!

React and Respond

Comprehension Check
Strategy: Text-to-Text Connections

The more you read, the more you will make text-to-text connections. You might be reading when you suddenly realize that the text reminds you of something else you read previously. As you read, try to make connections between the text and other books and articles, or even movies, scripts, and songs.

1. "The Legend of Bluebonnet" tells the story of a young girl's sacrifice. What other texts have you read about someone making a sacrifice for the good of the community?

2. In "The Apple King," the king hosts the Royal Apple Festival to honor the tree and share her fruit with cheerful company. What is another story that describes sharing with others? How does that story describe sharing differently?

3. "Lou Gehrig: The Luckiest Man" explains Gehrig's positive attitude toward life. Describe another story you have read about a person who maintained a positive attitude despite difficult odds.

4. "Queen Liliuokalani's Decision" explains her reasons for stepping down from the throne in Hawaii in order to keep peace. What are some other texts in which someone makes a personal sacrifice for the good of the people?

5. "Saving the Land" describes Roosevelt's love of nature and his preservation efforts. Why is it important to read about how to protect the environment?

Compare Texts
Make a Cause-and-Effect Chart

Think about the characters in each selection and how they showed integrity by making choices that are fair to all. Those actions (causes) and the results of those actions (effects) form cause-and-effect relationships. The Cause-and-Effect Chart at right shows how She-Who-Is-Alone's action affected her community. Copy and complete the chart by filling in the cause-and-effect relationships for the other characters in the selections you have read.

Showing Integrity

Cause		Effect
She-Who-Is-Alone sacrificed her beloved doll	→	The drought ended and bluebonnets filled the countryside.
The Apple King	→	
Lou Gehrig	→	
Queen Liliuokalani	→	
Theodore Roosevelt	→	

Character Development
Integrity

respect people with integrity because they
e choices that are fair to all.

es, people must make decisions that others disagree with.
careful work to try to make decisions that are fair to all.
the following situation. Think about what you would do,
a paragraph explaining your choice.

Mrs. Grunwell's class always play tag around the swingset
ess. However, Maria and Jen were hoping to play on the monkey
ecess. The boys use the monkey bars as the base for the game
d they run under the bars to get free. Maria and Jen worry that
get hurt or accidentally bump into the boys. Both groups decide
to come up with a compromise. What are some solutions the
night consider?

Technology
Role Models

Role models are people we look up to. These people usually have a lot of integrity, too. Think of someone you consider to be a role model. Draft an e-mail or letter telling the person what he or she means to you and why. Send it to the person if you can!

A

abdicated (ăb′ dĭ kā tĭd′) *v.* gave up power

absurd (əb sûrd′) *adj.* ridiculous; silly

accompany (ə kŭm′ pə nē) *v.* to go along with

accomplice (ə kŏm plĭs) *n.* someone who helps another do something wrong

alerted (ə lûr′ tĭd) *v.* notified; warned

ambitious (ăm bĭsh′ əs) *adj.* eager to achieve goals

amnesty (ăm′ nĭ stē) *n.* a pardon issued by a government, usually for political reasons

annexation (ăn′ ĭk sā′ shən) *n.* the addition of a smaller thing to a larger one, as a territory to a nation

ascend (ə sĕnd′) *v.* to move upward

B

balked (bôkt) *v.* stubbornly refused

blurted (blûr′ tĭd) *v.* said suddenly without thinking

bounty (boun′ tē) *n.* something given freely and abundantly

bustling (bŭs′ əl ĭng) *adj.* full of activity; busy

C

chasm (kăz′ əm) *n.* a deep crack or opening in Earth's surface

civilians (sĭ vĭl′ yənz) *n. pl.* people who are not active members in a military, police, or fire-fighting force

competent (kŏm′ pĭ tənt) *adj.* capable

confirmed (kən fûrmd′) *adj.* verified; proved

conservationists (kŏn′ sûr vā′ shən ĭstz) *n. pl.* people who promote using less of Earth's natural resources

contributions (kŏn′ trĭ byoō′ shənz) *n. pl.* donations or gifts

conundrum (kə nŭn′ drəm) *n.* a dilemma

courage (kûr′ ĭj) *n.* quality of mind or spirit that lets someone face danger or fear with bravery

courtiers (kôr′ tē ərz) *n. pl.* attendants in the royal court

crevasses (krĭ văs′ ĭz) *n. pl.* deep cracks

D

deployed (dĭ ploid′) *v.* sent off into action; launched

depose (dĭ pōz′) *v.* to remove from power

discipline (dĭs′ ə plĭn) *n.* controlled behavior

disentangling (dĭs′ ən tăng′ glĭng) *v.* undoing

dislodge (dĭs lŏj′) *v.* to remove

dispersed (dĭ spûrst′) *v.* scattered or moved apart

dispose (dĭ spōz′) *v.* to get rid of

distracted (dĭ străk′ tĭd) *adj.* having one's attention drawn to something else

disturbed (dĭ stûrbd′) *adj.* out of order; tampered with

drenched (drĕncht) *adj.* extremely wet

duplicate (doō′ plĭ kāt′) *v.* to copy; to repeat exactly

E

ecology (ĭ kŏl′ ə jē) *n.* the study of the relationships between organisms and th environments

elicited (ĭ lĭs′ ĭ tĭd) *v.* drew or received

epicenter (ĕp′ ĭ sĕn′ tər) *n.* the point surface right above the true center o earthquake

equestrian (ĭ kwĕs′ trē ən) *adj.* relating horseback riding

evacuated (ĭ văk′ yoō ā′ tĭd) *v.* left for s reasons

G

gossip (gŏs′ əp) *v.* to spread or listen to rumors about others

H

hailed (hāld) *v.* called out or signaled to

harrowing (hăr′ ō ĭng) *adj.* terribly scary

hurdled (hûr′ dld) *v.* leaped over

I

immensely (ĭ mĕns′ lē) *adv.* greatly

impaired (ĭm pârd′) *adj.* weakened in strength or quality

indisputable (ĭn′ dĭ spyo͞o′ tə bəl) *adj.* without doubt; undeniable

inlaid (ĭn′ lād′) *adj.* set as a design in a material such as wood

integrity (ĭn tĕg′ rĭ tē) *n.* the quality of maintaining high personal values

intended (ĭn tĕn′ dĭd) *v.* planned

intriguing (ĭn′ trēg′ ĭng) *adj.* exciting interest and curiosity

lavish (lăv′ ĭsh) *adj.* extravagant

luscious (lŭsh′ əs) *adj.* pleasant and sweet to taste and smell

magistrate (măj′ ĭ strāt′) *n.* a civil officer with authority to govern and enforce the law

marooned (mə ro͞ond′) *adj.* left alone with no hope of rescue or escape

materialized (mə tîr′ ē ə līzd) *v.* took shape

modest (mŏd′ ĭst) *adj.* humble

mutiny (myo͞ot′ n ē) *n.* a rebellion, usually of sailors against authority on a ship

PRONUNCIATION KEY

ă	pat	ŏ	pot	th	**th**in
ā	pay	ō	toe	*th*	**th**is
âr	care	ô	paw, for	hw	**wh**ich
ä	father	oi	n**oi**se	zh	vi**s**ion
ĕ	pet	ou	**ou**t	ə	**a**bout,
ē	be	o͝o	t**oo**k		**i**tem,
ĭ	pit	o͞o	b**oo**t		penc**i**l,
ī	pie	ŭ	cut		gall**o**p,
îr	pier	ûr	**ur**ge		circ**u**s

P

pharmaceutical companies (fär′ mə so͞o′ tĭ kəl kŭm′ pə nēz) *n. pl.* companies that manufacture medicinal drugs

pitched (pĭcht) *v.* dipped sharply back and forth in a rocking motion

preservationists (prĕz′ ər vā′ shə nĭsts) *n. pl.* people who promote protecting Earth's natural resources

priorities (prī ôr′ ĭ tēz) *n. pl.* the most important things one wants to accomplish or complete

prioritize (prī ôr′ ĭ tīz′) *v.* to arrange and do things in the order of importance

procession (prə sĕsh′ ən) *n.* a group of people walking in an orderly way

prototype (prō′ tə tīp′) *n.* an example or model

Q

quarrel (kwôr′ əl) *n.* an argument

queries (kwîr′ ēz) *n. pl.* questions

R

ranks (răngks) *v.* holds a specific position in order

remorseful (rĭ **môrs′** fəl) *adj.* deeply regretful

restore (rĭ **stôr′**) *v.* to bring back

retreat (rĭ **trēt′**) *n.* the act of withdrawing, usually from something unpleasant

retrieved (rĭ **trēvd′**) *v.* got back; recovered

ridiculous (rĭ **dĭk′** yə ləs) *adj.* very silly

rigorous (**rĭg′** ər əs) *adj.* harsh or trying

S

self-awareness (**sĕlf′** ə **wâr′** nĭs) *n.* awareness of one's personal feelings, behavior, and identity

smuggle (**smŭg′** əl) *v.* to transport secretly or illegally

stockades (stŏ **kādz′**) *n. pl.* enclosures used for prisoners

stranded (**străn′** dĭd) *adj.* left in a difficult situation alone or without help

T

teamwork (**tēm′** wûrk′) *n.* cooperative effort by the members of a group or team to achieve a common goal

U

unemployed (**ŭn′** ĕm **ploid′**) *adj.* without a job

V

veterans (**vĕt′** ər ənz) *n. pl.* people experienced in a specific field or activity

Text
p. 10 From *John Muir and Stickeen: An Icy Adventure with a No-Good Dog* by Julie Dunlap and Marybeth Lorbiecki, illustrated by Bill Farnsworth published by NorthWord Books for Young Readers. Reprinted by permission; **p. 16** Excerpt from *Amistad Rising: A Story of Freedom,* text Copyright © 1998 by Veronica Chambers, illustrations Copyright © 1998 by Paul Lee, reprinted by permission of Harcourt, Inc.; **p. 26** "Life Doesn't Frighten Me," Copyright © 1978 by Maya Angelou, from *And Still I Rise* by Maya Angelou. Used by permission of Random House, Inc.; **p. 36** From *The Hatmaker's Sign* retold by Candace Fleming, illustrated by Robert Andrew Parker. Text Copyright © 1998 by Candace Fleming. Illustrations Copyright © 1998 by Robert Andrew Parker. Reprinted by permission of Orchard Books, an imprint of Scholastic Inc.; **p. 44** From *The Rich Man and the Shoemaker* retold and illustrated by Bernadette Watts. Copyright © 2002 by NordSüd Verlag AG, Gossau Zürich, Switzerland. Reprinted by arrangement with North-South Books Inc., New York. All rights reserved; **p. 48** Excerpt from *The Great Escape Hat* by Tohby Riddle. Copyright © 2000 by Tohby Riddle. Reprinted by permission of Farrar, Straus & Giroux, LLC; **p. 66** From *Erandi's Braids* by Antonio Hernández Madrigal, illustrated by Tomie dePaola, copyright © 1999. Text copyright © 1999 Antonio Hernández Madrigal. Illustrations copyright © 1999 Tomie dePaola. Published by G.P. Putnam's Sons, a division of Penguin Putnam Books for Young Readers, A member of Penguin Group (USA) Inc., 345 Hudson Street, New York, NY 10014. All rights reserved; *The Moon Was at a Fiesta,* Revised Edition, by Matthew Gollub, illustrated by Leovigildo Martinez, 1997, Tortuga Press. Used by permission of Matthew Gollub; **p. 82** "Goha Gives His Son a Lesson About Life," from *Goha, the Wise Fool* retold by Denys Johnson-Davies, illustrated by Hany Ahmed and Hag Fattouh, Copyright © 2005 by Denys Johnson-Davies, text and Copyright © 2005 by Hany El Saed Ahmed and Hag Hamdy Mohamed Fattouh, illustrations. Used by permission of Philomel Books, A Division of Penguin Young Readers Group, A Member of Penguin Group (USA) Inc., 345 Hudson Street, New York, NY 10014. All rights reserved; **p. 92** From *The Island-below-the-Star,* written and illustrated by James Rumford. Copyright © 1998 by James Rumford. Reprinted by permission of Houghton Mifflin Company. All rights reserved; **p. 98** *Daisy's Garden* by Mordicai Gerstein and Susan Yard Harris. Reprinted by permission of: Mordicai Gerstein and Susan Yard Harris and their agents Raines & Raines. Text and illustrations © 1995 by Mordicai Gerstein and Susan Yard Harris; **p. 120** From *The Apple King* by Francesca Bosca and Giuliano Ferri. Copyright © 2001 by NordSüd Verlag AG, Gossau Zürich, Switzerland. Reprinted by arrangement with North-South Books, Inc., New York. All rights reserved; **p. 124** Excerpt from *Lou Gehrig: The Luckiest Man,* text Copyright © 1997 by David A. Adler, illustrations Copyright © 1997 by Terry Widener, reprinted by permission of Harcourt, Inc.

Photos
Cover © George C. Anderson; **pp. 8–9** © Maggie Hallahan/Corbis; **p. 22** Courtesy of Library of Congress; **p. 24** © AP Photo; **p. 25** © Getty Images; **p. 26** © Joel W. Rogers/Corbis; **pp. 28–29** © Jupiter Images; **p. 30** (top) Courtesy of Library of Congress; **p. 30** (bottom) © Jupiter Images; **p. 32** Courtesy of Library of Congress; **pp. 34–35** © Royalty-Free/Corbis; **pp. 54–57** © AP Photo; **p. 59** © Stefano Bianchetti/Corbis; **pp. 64–65** © Royalty-Free/Corbis; **p. 74** Courtesy of Intel; **p. 75** © Photodisc; **p. 83** © Sarah Gauch **p. 84** Courtesy of NASA; **p. 85** (top) Courtesy of NASA; **p. 85** (bottom) © Photodisc; **p. 86** Courtesy of NASA; **p. 87** (top) © Photodisc; **p. 87** (bottom) © Getty Images; **p. 88** Courtesy of NASA; **pp. 90–91** © Handout/Reuters/Corbis; **p. 102** Courtesy of NOAA; **pp. 103–104** © AP Photo; **p. 105** © Photodisc; **pp. 106–108** Eileen Ryan; **p. 110** ©